Dinopedia

THE COMPLETE GUIDE TO EVERYTHING DINOSAUR

With an introduction by Dr. Joseph Sertich,
Curator of Vertebrate Paleontology, Denver Museum of Nature & Science

Publisher: Jim Childs
Vice President and Associate Publisher: Margot Schupf
Vice President, Finance: Vandana Patel
Executive Director, Marketing Services: Carol Pittard
Executive Director, Business Development: Suzanne Albert
Executive Director, Marketing: Susan Hettleman
Publishing Director: Megan Pearlman
Associate Director of Publicity: Courtney Greenhalgh
Associate General Counsel: Simone Procas
Assistant Director, Special Sales: Ilene Schreider
Senior Marketing Manager, Sales Marketing: Danielle Costa
Associate Production Manager: Kimberly Marshall
Associate Prepress Manager: Alex Voznesenskiy
Associate Project Manager: Stephanie Braga

Editorial Director: Stephen Koepp
Senior Editor: Roe D'Angelo
Children's Editor: Jonathan White
Copy Chief: Rina Bander
Design Manager: Anne-Michelle Gallero
Editorial Operations: Gina Scauzillo

Special Thanks: Katherine Barnet, Brad Beatson, Jeremy Biloon,
Susan Chodakiewicz, Rose Cirrincione, Assu Etsubneh, Mariana Evans,
Christine Font, Hillary Hirsch, David Kahn, Jean Kennedy, Amy Mangus,
Courtney Mifsud, Nina Mistry, Dave Rozzelle, Matthew Ryan,
Ricardo Santiago, Divyam Shrivastava, Adriana Tierno

Published by Time Home Entertainment Inc.
1271 Avenue of the Americas, 6th floor • New York, NY 10020

ISBN 10: 1-61893-357-4
ISBN 13: 978-1-61893-357-7

We welcome your comments and suggestions about
Time Home Entertainment Books. Please write to us at:
Time Home Entertainment Books, Attention: Book Editors,
P.O. Box 11016, Des Moines, IA 50336-1016

If you would like to order any of our hardcover Collector's Edition books,
please call us at 1-800-327-6388, Monday through Friday, 7 a.m. to 8 p.m.,
or Saturday, 7 a.m. to 6 p.m., Central Time.

Produced by

President: Susan Knopf
Writer and Image Manager: Lori Stein
Special Advisor: Dr. Joseph Sertich, Curator of Vertebrate Paleontology,
Denver Museum of Nature & Science
Editor: Beth Sutinis
Copyeditor: Stephanie Engel
Editorial Intern: Brittany Gialanella
Designed by: Andrij Borys Associates, LLC
Designers: Andrij Borys and Iwona Usakiewicz
Associate Designer: Mia Balaquiot
Special Thanks: Chelsea Burris, Michael Centore, Leslie Garisto.

MEET THE EXPERT

I have been fascinated by dinosaurs and their world my entire life. As a kid, I spent hours searching for fossils anywhere I could, occasionally picking up a piece of fossilized seashell or shark tooth but never making the truly big discovery—a new dinosaur. Now, after years of hard work and research, my job is to do just that.

From the frozen islands of Antarctica to the sand dunes of Egypt to the forests of Madagascar, I've had the privilege not only of traveling the globe, but also of traveling back in time. When I crack open a rock to reveal a fossil, I can't help but feel transported back to the dinosaur's mysterious world, and I picture the living, breathing animal in its ecosystem. Dinosaur paleontology is the perfect combination of biology, geology, and detective work.

Rather than seeing dinosaurs as museum objects, paleontologists view dinosaurs as fascinating creatures with behaviors as complex as those of any living animal. Though the dinosaur fossil record is limited mostly to bones and tracks, we now have amazing tools for understanding dinosaurs as real animals. Many of the facts you will encounter in this book are based on current scientific thinking. However, some of them will likely be proven wrong in the coming decades, overturned by new discoveries and advancements in technology. This is what makes paleontology such a captivating and dynamic science; the future of dinosaur paleontology is as bright as ever.

As a dinosaur curator at a museum, I am often asked: Haven't all the dinosaurs already been discovered? The science of dinosaur paleontology is over 170 years old, but the number of known species has nearly doubled in the past 20 years. If anything, we are only just scratching the surface of dinosaur discoveries, with thousands of new species waiting for a whole new generation of paleontologists to discover!

Dr. Joseph Sertich, Dinosaur Paleontologist
Curator of Vertebrate Paleontology, Denver Museum of Nature & Science

ABOUT THIS BOOK

Millions of years ago, some of the most amazing animals that ever existed ruled the earth. While the Age of Dinosaurs ended 66 million years ago, when all the dinosaurs died out, we are still learning new things about dinosaurs all the time. *Dinopedia* is the ultimate book about these incredible creatures.

Dinosaurs came in many different shapes and sizes, and they lived all around the world and in every habitat. Some were fast and vicious meat eaters; others were gentle giants that munched on leaves at the tops of tall trees. Some had horns on their heads or spikes on their shoulders or backs, some were covered with feathers, and some had hundreds of teeth embedded in their cheeks. There were dinosaurs with long, thin tails, and some with clublike tails that they swung around to attack others or defend themselves.

Inside, you'll read about how meat-eating dinosaurs like *Tyrannosaurus rex* hunted and killed their prey, and how giant sauropods like *Brachiosaurus* ate rocks to help them digest the huge amount of leaves they needed to eat to survive. You'll learn about dinosaurs that could fly, and others that could swim. In the hundreds of beautiful illustrations and photos, you'll see how dinosaurs moved, gave birth to and raised their young, and defended themselves. You'll discover which were the longest, the shortest, the fastest, and the slowest—the record breakers of the dinosaur world. And you'll find out about "living dinosaurs," animals alive today that are little changed from their prehistoric ancestors. Look for "On the Scene" features to journey back in time and imagine what dinosaur lives were really like. And follow the "Dino Detective" boxes to learn all about discovering dinosaur fossils.

Along the way, Dr. Joseph Sertich will be your guide. He is an experienced paleontologist (that means he's a dinosaur expert). He has worked with thousands of dinosaur fossils and made many new discoveries in the field. He brings this hands-on expertise to the pages of *Dinopedia*. Look for special notes from him where you see "Dr. Joe Says."

You can read this book from front to back, or dip in anywhere—every page is filled with fascinating facts and photos about dinosaurs and other prehistoric animals. Check out "Dinosaur Taxonomy" and "Dinosaur Anatomy" first and you'll learn things that will help you enjoy the rest of the book. With pronunciation guides for more than 750 known dinosaurs, *Dinopedia* will make you an instant expert! First, let's look at how big dinosaurs really were.

DINOSAUR SIZES

Many people think of dinosaurs as huge animals and some of them were astonishingly huge—the largest animals to ever walk on land. But there were also small and medium-size dinosaurs. Every chapter in this book is introduced by a chart that lists all the dinosaurs in every category and notes their size, from XS for extra small to XXL for extra, extra large. Here's a guide that gives you an idea what those sizes mean.

Length from tip of snout to tip of tail

XS Under 5 feet: *Archaeopteryx*

S 5-10 feet: *Deinonychus*

M 10-20 feet: *Zuniceratops*

L 20-30 feet: *Stegosaurus*

XL 30-40 feet: *Yangchuanosaurus*

XXL Over 40 feet: *Brachiosaurus*

Humans average 5.5 feet in height

Contents

Planet Earth is about 4.6 billion years old. For the first few billion years, Earth's atmosphere had little oxygen, and almost no life could be supported. Over time, the air became more livable and small creatures appeared. Eventually, after millions of years, they became bigger and more like animals that are alive today. The earliest known creatures lived in water; as they evolved, some moved to land. Then, 252 million years ago, dinosaurs appeared, and what is known as the Age of Dinosaurs began.

SHIFTING CONTINENTS

During the Age of Dinosaurs, Earth did not look the way it does today.

Pangaea

At the beginning, there was one big landmass called Pangaea (pan-JEE-uh). Huge bodies of water flowed over large sections of the land.

Laurasia and Gondwana

Over hundreds of millions of years, Pangaea broke into two large landmasses: Laurasia (the northern part) and Gondwana (the southern part). Scientists think that the first dinosaurs appeared in Gondwana.

Continents form

Eventually, as the landmasses continued to shift, the continents we know today began to take shape.

Modern World

Today, there are seven continents on Earth. The equator (marked in red) is an imaginary line around the middle that separates north from south.

4.6
BILLION YEARS AGO
Earth was created.

3.8
BILLION YEARS AGO
Life on Earth begins.

No one has yet proven how the universe was formed. The leading scientific theory is that extreme heat caused explosions and from this event the planets, including Earth, were formed.

Cave painting in Algeria

LEARNING ABOUT THE PREHISTORIC PAST

About 40,000 years ago, primitive humans began recording the events of their lives, first in drawings, and later in words. That was the beginning of history. Everything before that is prehistory. We have to find clues in leftovers from the animals, rocks, and plants that lived during the years before recorded history in order to know what was going on.

THE AGE OF DINOSAURS

For about 186 million years—less than five percent of the time that Earth has been in existence—a group of extraordinary creatures dominated our planet. This was the Age of Dinosaurs, a time when thousands of different reptiles—large and small, gentle and fierce—lived, ate, fought, raised families, and evolved into powerful animals with strange and diverse features. Dinosaurs no longer exist, but evidence of them survived as fossils. Finding and studying these fossils allows us to learn about the dinosaurs and the world they lived in.

66 MILLION YEARS AGO
Mammals and animals thrived after dinosaurs died out.

252–66 MILLION YEARS AGO
The Age of Dinosaurs.

200,000–PRESENT
Humans appeared 200,000 years ago. This time span is such a small part Earth's existence, it's too small to show here.

A Prehistoric Timeline

Scientists have divided time into eras and periods. An era is very long stretch of time that corresponds with important changes in the world. Eras are divided into periods, in which the changes are not as significant.

PRECAMBRIAN ERA

4.6 BILLION YEARS AGO
The sun became very hot, causing the stars around it to collide and explode. One of the rocks created in this explosion was Earth.

2.5 BILLION YEARS AGO
Oxygen levels on Earth rose. Oxygen was probably emitted by prehistoric plants.

PALEOZOIC ERA

545 MILLION YEARS AGO
Very primitive shellfish—similar to snails and clams—appeared in warm waters all over Earth.

530 MILLION YEARS AGO
The earliest vertebrates—animals with backbones—appeared.

430 MILLION YEARS AGO
Large, spiderlike creatures that lived in the ocean began to move to land. At the same time, plants began to grow on land.

370 MILLION YEARS AGO
Amphibians—animals that could live both in water and on land—emerged from the water. *Tiktaalik*, which looked a little like a crocodile, may have been the first one.

300 MILLION YEARS AGO
The first reptiles were similar to small lizards. In the first few million years, they grew bigger and walked on land. Over the next 50 million years, they dominated the world; many are alive today, including turtles, snakes, and birds.

MESOZOIC ERA

252–201 MILLION YEARS AGO
TRIASSIC PERIOD The first dinosaurs appeared, mostly small carnivores, in what is now South America.

201–144 MILLION YEARS AGO
JURASSIC PERIOD Huge dinosaurs ruled the world, and small, furry mammals appeared. Flowering plants appeared and became a food supply for herbivores.

144–66 MILLION YEARS AGO
CRETACEOUS PERIOD Dinosaurs continued to dominate. Then, 66 million years ago, dinosaurs became extinct. No one knows exactly why, but it was likely because a huge asteroid hit Earth.

CENOZOIC ERA

66 MILLION YEARS AGO–PRESENT
Large mammals appeared. The first two-legged humanlike creature appeared about 3.5 to 4 million years ago. The first modern human appeared about 200,000 years ago. We are still in the Cenozoic era.

DINOSAURS BY PERIOD

Dinosaurs didn't all live in the same period of time. During the 186 million years of the Age of Dinosaurs, groups lived and died out as others evolved. Each period lasted millions of years, so not all of these dinosaurs bumped into one another, even if they lived in the same period. Here are some of the dinosaurs that lived in each period.

LATE TRIASSIC
227 TO 201 MILLION YEARS AGO

Camposaurus

Coelophysis

Eoraptor

Herrerasaurus

Mussaurus

Staurikosaurus

LATE JURASSIC
159 TO 144 MILLION YEARS AGO

Allosaurus

Apatosaurus

Brachiosaurus

Ceratosaurus

Diplodocus

Stegosaurus

EARLY JURASSIC
201 TO 180 MILLION YEARS AGO

Anchisaurus

Barapasaurus

Cryolophosaurus

Heterodontosaurus

Massospondylus

Scelidosaurus

EARLY CRETACEOUS
144 TO 98 MILLION YEARS AGO

Caudipteryx

Compsognathus

Deinonychus

Microraptor

Paralatitan

Sauropelta

MIDDLE JURASSIC
180 TO 159 MILLION YEARS AGO

Amygdalodon

Cetiosaurus

Huayangosaurus

Megalosaurus

Shunosaurus

Thescelosaurus

LATE CRETACEOUS
98 TO 66 MILLION YEARS AGO

Alamosaurus

Ankylosaurus

Pachycephalosaurus

Parasaurolopholous

Triceratops

Tyrannosaurus rex

What Is a Fossil?

Dinosaurs died out millions of years ago, but their fossils remain. How is that possible? Fossils formed when a creature died in a place that had the right amount of water and silt (bits of sand or clay in water) to bury the bones quickly. As the skin and flesh decayed, or rotted away, silt settled on the bones and protected and preserved them. Once this process took place, bones could stay undisturbed for millions of years.

CASTS AND IMPRESSIONS

Dinosaur leftovers can be useful even if they are no longer there. If a dinosaur died on a soft surface, such as clay or silt, its body might have left a space or impression. Researchers can fill that space with plaster and create a cast (shown at left) that shows the size and shape of the body or its parts.

FOSSIL FORMS

Leftovers from the prehistoric world come in many forms. Each one adds to our knowledge of what was going on millions of years ago.

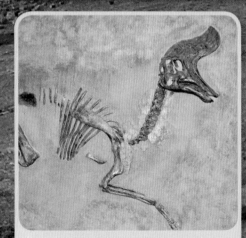

SKELETONS Scientists can learn a great deal from complete or partial skeletons that are found with most of the bones still in position.

BONES, SKULLS, AND TEETH Putting smaller pieces together gives clues as to how the rest of a skeleton may have looked.

EGGS AND NESTS Scientists have learned a lot about how dinosaur babies were born from fossilized nests and eggs.

A **paleontologist** (PAY-lee-on-TAH-luh-jist) studies fossils to learn about prehistoric life. *Paleo* means very, very old; *ologist* refers to someone who studies something.

An expert can make a good estimate of how big a dinosaur was even if only one bone is found, and some dinosaurs have been identified from a single bone or tooth. On this dig, several *T. rex* bones were found.

SKIN AND FEATHERS
Though hard to come by—because soft materials such as skin and feathers rarely became fossils—some finds show what the outsides of dinosaurs looked like.

COPROLITES
Dinosaur droppings that became fossilized give researchers clues about what dinosaurs ate. *Coprolite* is a fancy word for poop.

TRACKS AND FOOTPRINTS
By measuring fossilized impressions of dinosaur feet, experts can figure out how big a dinosaur was and how fast it walked or ran.

Discovering Dinosaurs

...le have been discovering dinosaur bones for thousands of years, but at first no one knew what they ... . About 200 years ago, people began to recognize them as something other than bones from mysterious ...ts" or "dragons" and gave them scientific names. The first nearly complete dinosaur skeleton ever ...d was discovered in 1858 by William Parker Foulke on a farm in Haddonfield, New Jersey. The 30-foot ...eton, which was missing its skull, was named *Hadrosaurus foulkii* ("Foulke's big lizard").

DINO DETECTIVES

Paleontologists decipher clues from fossils. Fossils are bones that have survived for millions of years because all the soft tissue in them has been replaced by silt. Paleontologists develop skills that help them find and analyze these fossils so that they can learn how dinosaurs lived and how their bodies worked.

DINO DETECTIVE

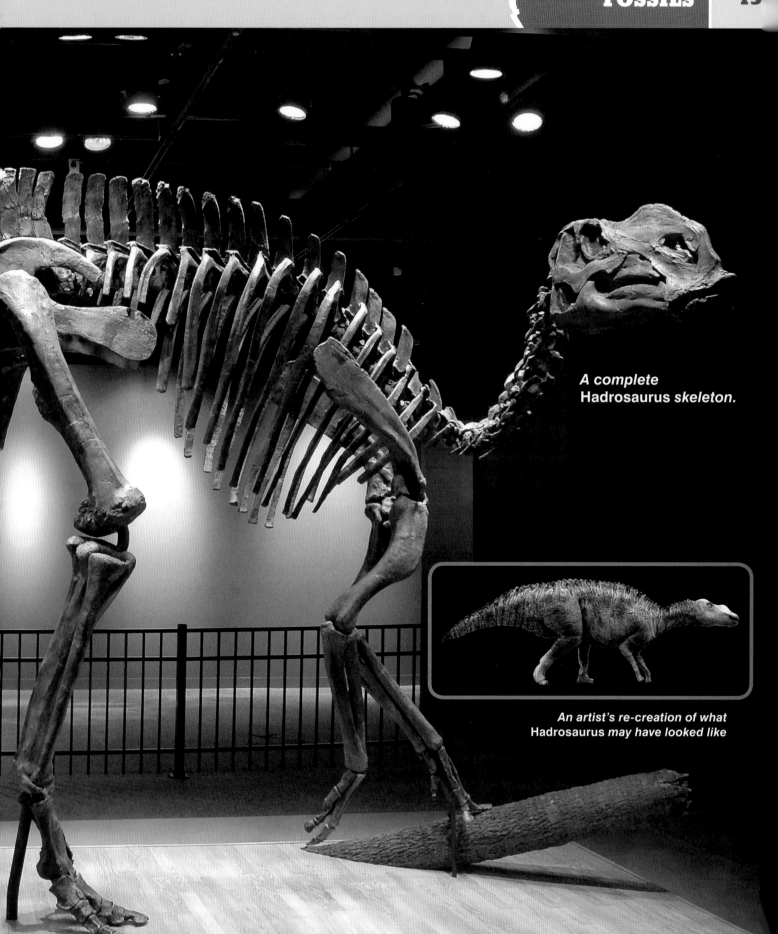

A complete Hadrosaurus *skeleton.*

An artist's re-creation of what Hadrosaurus *may have looked like*

What Is a Dinosaur?

In the 1700s, a man named Carl Linnaeus organized all living things into groups so that scientists could better understand how they were related to one another. The system of organizing and classifying living things is called taxonomy; his system specifically is called Linnaean taxonomy.

TAXONOMY

Large groups whose members share a few common features are called classes. Animals with more features in common are organized into smaller groups called orders and suborders. Within each order, animals are sorted into families that have even more common features. In each family, there are genera (that's the plural of genus); a genus is a group of animals that are very similar. Finally, a group in which all the animals are nearly the same is called a species. We know most dinosaurs by their genus names, like *Stegosaurus* and *Apatosaurus*. A dinosaur with a double name was a particular species within a genus—for example, *Tyrannosaurus rex* was a species of the genus *Tyrannosaurus*.

WHAT MAKES A DINOSAUR A DINOSAUR?

Dinosaurs came in different forms—just a few inches long or well over 100 feet, walking on two legs or four, eating meat or plants. But they all had certain common features.

▶ **A HOLE IN THE HIP** Every dinosaur had a hole through its hip socket.
▶ **UPRIGHT POSTURE** Dinosaurs could stand up straight, that made many of them able to run fast.
▶ **TWO PALATES** Their mouths were structured so they could eat and breathe at the same time.
▶ **HOLES IN THE HEAD** Their skulls had three pairs of openings in addition to the eyes and nostrils.

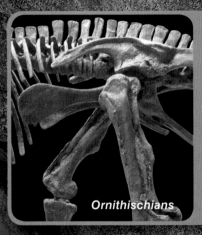

Ornithischians

TWO ORDERS OF DINOSAUR, PLEASE!

Some dinosaurs had hip bones that pointed backward, while on others these bones radiated away from the hips. Dinosaurs are classified in two orders based on this difference. The dinosaurs with hip bones that pointed backward are called ornithischians, or bird-hipped dinosaurs. The ones with bones that radiated away from the hips are called saurischians, or lizard-hipped dinosaurs.

Saurischians

DINOSAURIA

In 1842, scientist Sir Richard Owen decided that a new class was needed for fossils of several large animals that did not fit into any other group. He established the class of Dinosauria, which contained only three dinosaur genera at that time: *Megalosaurus*, *Iguanodon*, and *Hylaeosaurus*. As many more fossils were found, Dinosauria was divided into smaller groups.

THE FIVE DINOSAUR SUBORDERS

THEROPODS
SAURISCHIAN ORDER
This diverse group included huge apex predators such as *Tyrannosaurus rex* and small, birdlike creatures such as *Troodon*.

SAUROPODS
SAURISCHIAN ORDER
These group of quadrupedal herbivores, with which included *Brachiosaurus* and *Apatosaurus*, grew very large.

THYREOPHORANS
ORNITHISCHIAN ORDER
These dinosaurs were large, heavy quadrupeds with bony plates arranged on their bodies, such as *Stegosaurus* and *Ankylosaurus*.

ORNITHOPODS
ORNITHISCHIAN ORDER
The dinosaurs in this group, which included *Iguanodon* and *Hadrosaurus*, could switch from walking on four legs while they browsed for food to running from predators on two legs.

MARGINOCEPHA
ORNITHISCHIAN ORD
group included ceratopsi pointy horns, such as *Tri* and thick-headed dinosa bony caps on their skulls *Stegoceras*.

Theropods, the predators that ruled the planet during the Age of Dinosaurs, ranged from little *Troodon* to supersize *Spinosaurus*. When the largest ones stomped around, the ground trembled and smaller animals fled in fear. The first of these 267 known dinosaurs were small compared to later dinosaurs, but even the earliest ones had big, sharp teeth for eating meat.

All theropods walked on two feet. Many had birdlike bodies with hollow bones, which made them light and fast. Other theropods, like *Tyrannosaurus rex* and *Giganotosaurus*, were heavy and slow. All of them had eyes and brains that were larger than those of other creatures at that time. Better brainpower and sharp vision helped theropods hunt and avoid attacks.

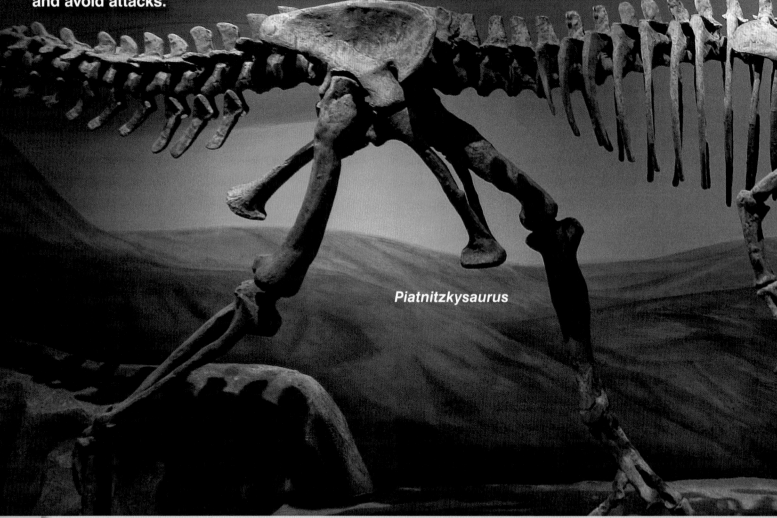

Piatnitzkysaurus

LATE TRIASSIC

227 TO 201
MILLION YEARS AGO

Herrerasaurus, *Staurikosaurus*, and other theropods with dinosaur features appeared. They were not apex predators in this age; other huge reptiles dominated.

EARLY JURASSIC

201 TO 180
MILLION YEARS AGO

Small and medium-size theropods roamed Earth. Many other predators became extinct while dinosaurs, including *Coelophysis*, dominated.

MIDDLE JURASSIC

180 TO 159
MILLION YEARS AGO

By the end of this period, there were four kinds of theropods: ceratosaurs, megalosaurs, allosaurs, and coelurosaurs. Birds evolved from small, nonflying dinosaurs.

Theropods

▶ Sharp teeth curved inward and had serrated, or sawlike, edges.

▶ Sharp claws were used to stab prey and hold it in place for eating.

AT A GLANCE

The name *theropod* comes from from a Greek word meaning "beast feet." Theropod fossils have been found on all seven continents. There are 267 known theropods.

Theropods were:
➡ part of the saurischian (lizard-hipped) order of dinosaurs
➡ bipedal
➡ carnivores; some also ate fish, insects, and plants

Theropods are divided into five sections in this book:

Early Theropods
➡ Had sharp teeth
➡ Were smaller than later theropods

Jurassic Theropods
➡ Lived during the Jurassic period
➡ Grew to 40 feet or more

Feathered Theropods
➡ Had hollow bones
➡ Some were small and birdlike; others were huge

Near-Raptors
➡ Had wings and feathers
➡ Were similar to birds

Paravians
➡ Also known as avian dinosaurs
➡ Some flew

Some well-known theropods: *Allosaurus, Oviraptor, T. rex*

LATE JURASSIC	EARLY CRETACEOUS	LATE CRETACEOUS
159 TO 144 **MILLION YEARS AGO**	**144 TO 98** **MILLION YEARS AGO**	**98 TO 66** **MILLION YEARS AGO**
The evolutionary changes of some theropod dinosaurs, such as *Archaeopteryx*, included feathers and wings that made it possible for them to fly.	Theropods dominated: allosaurs and coelurosaurs in the Northern Hemisphere (north of the equator), spinosaurs and ceratosaurs in the Southern Hemisphere.	*Tyrannosaurus rex* was one of the last dinosaurs to appear, near the end of this period and about 2 million years before all dinosaurs became extinct.

EARLIEST THEROPODS

	SIZE	AGE	FOSSILS	LOCATION
Chindesaurus (chin-dee-**SORE**-us)	S	LT	Bone	NA
Daemonosaurus (day-mon-oh-**SORE**-us)	S	LT	Partial skeleton	NA
Herrerasaurus (huh-rare-uh-**SORE**-us)	M	LT	Skull	SA
Staurikosaurus (stah-**RIH**-koh-sore-us)	S	LT	Full skeleton	SA
Tawa (**TAH**-wah)	M	LT	Full skeleton	NA

COELOPHYSOIDS

	SIZE	AGE	FOSSILS	LOCATION
Camposaurus (**CAM**-poh-sore-us)	S	LT	Partial skeleton	NA
Coelophysis (see-lo-**FIE**-sis)	S	LT	Full skeleton	NA
Liliensternus (lih-lee-en-**STERN**-us)	M	LT	Full skeleton	EU
Lophostropheus (lo-foe-**STROH**-fee-us)	M	LT	Partial skeleton	EU
Megapnosaurus (muh-**GAP**-no-sore-us)	S	LT/EJ	Skull	AF/NA
Podokesaurus (**PO-DO**-kuh-**SORE**-us)	XS	EJ	Partial skeleton	NA
Procompsognathus (pro-**COMP**-sug-nay-thus)	XS	LT	Partial skeleton	EU
Segisaurus (**SEHG**-ee-sore-us)	XS	EJ	Skull	NA

CRESTED DINOSAURS

	SIZE	AGE	FOSSILS	LOCATION
Cryolophosaurus (**CRY**-oh-loh-foe-sore-us)	M	EJ	Skull, Partial skeleton	AN
Dilophosaurus (die-loh-foe-**SORE**-us)	M	EJ	Full skeleton	NA/AS
Dracovenator (**DRAY**-koh-vee-nay-tore)	M	EJ	Skull	AF
Sinosaurus (sine-oh-**SORE**-us)	S	EJ	Teeth	AS
Zupaysaurus (zoo-pay-**SORE**-us)	M	LT	Skull	SA

CERATOSAURS

	SIZE	AGE	FOSSILS	LOCATION
Berberosaurus (bur-bear-oh-**SORE**-us)	M	EJ	Partial skeleton	AF
Camarillasaurus (cam-uh-rill-uh-**SORE**-us)	UN	EC	Partial skeleton	EU
Ceratosaurus (sir-**RAT**-uh-sore-us)	M	LJ	Full skeleton	NA/AF
Deltadromeus (del-ta-**DROH**-mee-us)	L	LC	Partial skeleton	AF
Elaphrosaurus (ee-**LAH**-froh-sore-us)	M	LJ	Partial skeleton	AF
Eoabelisaurus (**EE**-oh-ah-bell-ih-sore-us)	L	MJ	Full skeleton	SA
Genyodectes (jen-ee-oh-**DEK**-teez)	L	EC	Teeth, Partial skeleton	SA
Limusaurus (lee-moo-**SORE**-us)	S	MJ	Full skeleton	AS
Spinostropheus (**SPY**-no-stroh-fee-us)	S	EC	Partial skeleton	AF

ABELISAURS

	SIZE	AGE	FOSSILS	LOCATION
Abelisaurus (ah-bel-ee-**SORE**-us)	L	LC	Skull	SA
Arcovenator (**ARK**-oh-ven-ay-tore)	M	LC	Teeth, Partial skeleton	EU
Aucasaurus (**AW**-kuh-sore-us)	M	LC	Full skeleton	SA
Carnotaurus (kar-no-**TORE**-us)	L	LC	Full skeleton	SA
Dahalokely (dah-ha-loh-**KEH**-lee)	M	LC	Partial skeleton	AF
Ekrixinatosaurus (ek-**RIKS**-ee-na-toe-sore-us)	M	LC	Full skeleton	SA
Ilokelesia (**EYE**-loh-keh-lee-zha)	L	LC	Partial skeleton	SA
Indosaurus (in-doh-**SORE**-us)	M	LC	Skull	AS
Kryptops (**KRIP**-tops)	L	EC	Partial skeleton	AF
Majungasaurus (mah-**JUN**-gah-sore-us)	L	LC	Teeth, Partial skeleton	AF
Masiakasaurus (**MAH**-she-ah-kah-sore-us)	S	LC	Partial skeleton	SA
Noasaurus (**NOH**-ah-sore-us)	S	LC	Partial skeleton	SA
Pycnonemosaurus (**PIK**-no-neh-mo-sore-us)	L	LC	Partial skeleton	SA
Quilmesaurus (keel-may-**SORE**-us)	M	LC	Partial skeleton	SA
Rahiolisaurus (rah-hee-**OH**-lee-sore-us)	L	LC	Partial skeleton	AS
Rajasaurus (rah-jah-**SORE**-us)	L	LC	Partial skeleton	AS
Rugops (**ROO**-gops)	L	LC	Skull	AF
Skorpiovenator (skor-pee-oh-**VEN**-a-tore)	L	LC	Full skeleton	SA
Velocisaurus (veh-**LOSS**-ih-sore-us)	XS	LC	Partial skeleton	SA
Xenotarsosaurus (**ZEEN**-oh-tar-soh-sore-us)	L	LC	Partial skeleton	SA

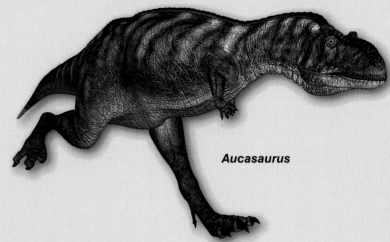

Aucasaurus

LEGEND

Featured dinosaurs are set in red in the list above.

SIZE
- XS — Under 5 feet
- S — 5-10 feet
- M — 10-20 feet
- L — 20-30 feet
- XL — 30-40 feet
- XXL — Over 40 feet
- UN — Unknown

AGE (years ago)
- LT — Late Triassic (227-201 million)
- EJ — Early Jurassic (201-180 million)
- MJ — Middle Jurassic (180-159 million)
- LJ — Late Jurassic (159-144 million)
- EC — Early Cretaceous (144-98 million)
- LC — Late Cretaceous (98-66 million)

FOSSILS
- Full skeleton
- Partial skeleton
- Skull
- Bone
- Teeth

LOCATION
- AS — Asia
- AF — Africa
- EU — Europe
- AU — Australia
- NA — North America
- SA — South America
- AN — Antarctica

Early Theropods
Herrerasaurs, Coelophysoids, Ceratosaurs, and Their Relatives

Majungasaurus,
a large theropod of the
Late Cretaceous period

The earliest theropods were also the earliest dinosaurs, and they weren't much like the huge carnivores to come. They did, however, have features that made them able to compete with other animals in their environments: very sharp teeth and claws, strong legs, and hollow bones that made them light enough to run quickly. These animals, including *Herrerasaurus* and *Tawa*—which lived during the Late Triassic period (227-201 million years ago)—were primitive versions of the theropod dinosaurs that followed them.

Theropods were diverse. They came in many different sizes, from under 3 feet to more than 45 feet long. Some had long, curving necks and tails and jaws shaped like a crocodile's; others had shorter necks, tails, and snouts. But they all were bipedal (they walked on two feet), ate meat (some ate other food as well), and had hollow bones. By the Middle Jurassic period, the earliest theropods had disappeared. Most of the later ones were large, and some had developed interesting growths, such as crests and horns, on their heads.

HERRERASAURUS

➡ A bipedal carnivore that ate small and medium-size prey

➡ Named for Don Victorino Herrera, an Andean rancher who discovered the first fossils

➡ Was about 12 feet long; weighed more than 200 pounds

➡ Had hinged jaws and jagged-edged teeth

FUN FACT *Herrerasaurus* was one of the earliest dinosaurs ever found.

LILIENSTERNUS

➡ A bipedal carnivore that ate smaller, plant-eating dinosaurs

➡ Named for paleontologist Hugo Rühle von Lilienstern

➡ Was about 15 feet long; weighed nearly 300 pounds

➡ Had five fingers on each hand

FUN FACT *Liliensternus* may have been able to store fat to help it survive when food was scarce.

CERATOSAURUS

➡ A bipedal carnivore, big and strong enough to kill even large sauropods

➡ Named for the horn on its face (*cera* comes from the Greek word for "horn")

➡ Was up to 20 feet long; weighed 1,000–2,000 pounds

➡ Had a sharp horn over its nose, two hard and pointy horns over its eyes, and small bony plates running down its spine

FUN FACT *Ceratosaurus* is the only theropod known to have this full range of body armor, though others had horns.

DILOPHOSAURUS

➡ A bipedal carnivore, thought to be a fast runner

➡ Named for the two round crests on its head (*di* means "two" and *lophos* means "crest" in Greek)

➡ Was about 20 feet long; weighed more than 1,000 pounds

➡ Had three fingers on each hand and four toes on each back foot

FUN FACT *Dilophosaurus* had a weak jaw for a carnivore, and some experts think it was a scavenger, feasting on animals that were already dead.

Coelophysis: Hollow Form

This birdlike dinosaur was lightweight and graceful, with a long neck and tail. It was also fast and deadly and had many razor-sharp teeth that it used to eat smaller reptiles. Its eyes were exceptionally large, even for a theropod, making it a good hunter.

Scientists think that *Coelophysis* usually hunted alone or in small groups and only formed large packs when food was scarce. When their usual prey was not available, several of them would gang up on larger animals and share the meat. *Coelophysis* skeletons have been found grouped together, which is evidence that they may have traveled in packs.

PALEO DATA

COELOPHYSIS

PRONUNCIATION
see-lo-FIE-sis

SIZE
About 9 feet long and 3 feet tall; weighed 40 pounds (about the length of a small horse, but much lighter)

AGE
Late Triassic, about 210 million years ago

LOCATION
Southwestern United States

FOSSILS
Many complete skeletons

DIET
Meat

WISHBONE

A wishbone is a small bone between the neck and shoulders of a bird. The wishbone makes the shoulders strong and flexible; it acts as a spring to help birds take off and fly. *Coelophysis* was one of the first dinosaurs that had a wishbone. This springy bone added strength to the dinosaur's shoulders when it was using its arms.

SAURUS STORY

FOSSIL FILE

By studying *Coelophysis*'s footprints, which were just 4 inches long, and the spaces between them, scientists have determined that these dinosaurs moved fast. Their hollow bones made them lightweight and swift, and their name even means "hollow form."

FLASH FLOOD AT GHOST RANCH

Ghost Ranch is an area in New Mexico where many dinosaur fossils have been found, including hundreds of full and partial *Coelophysis* skeletons in huge, tangled piles. In the Triassic period, the area that is now Ghost Ranch was located near the equator. Scientists think monsoons could have caused flash floods that trapped and drowned a whole pack of these dinosaurs. Today, Ghost Ranch is a vacation resort and artists' colony.

The Body of the Beast

Experts have a good idea of how dinosaur bones fit together, because full skeletons of many species have been found. There are key variations in certain body parts in different types of dinosaurs. This skeleton shows one particular combination of body parts, and the descriptions explain the variations.

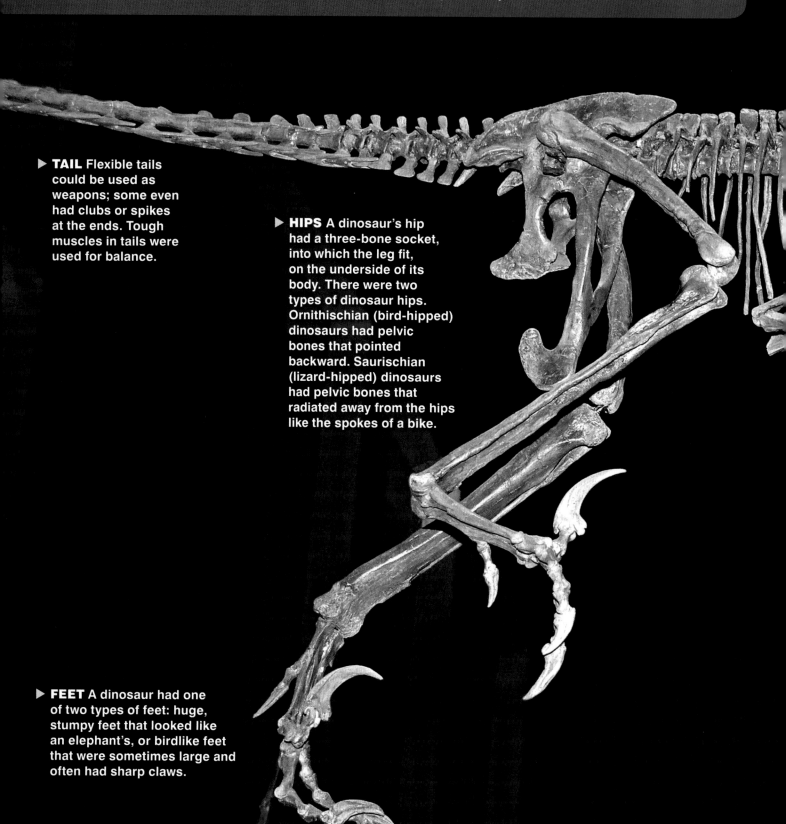

▶ **TAIL** Flexible tails could be used as weapons; some even had clubs or spikes at the ends. Tough muscles in tails were used for balance.

▶ **HIPS** A dinosaur's hip had a three-bone socket, into which the leg fit, on the underside of its body. There were two types of dinosaur hips. Ornithischian (bird-hipped) dinosaurs had pelvic bones that pointed backward. Saurischian (lizard-hipped) dinosaurs had pelvic bones that radiated away from the hips like the spokes of a bike.

▶ **FEET** A dinosaur had one of two types of feet: huge, stumpy feet that looked like an elephant's, or birdlike feet that were sometimes large and often had sharp claws.

Hundreds of thousands of fossilized dinosaur bones and teeth have been discovered over time. By studying these fossils, scientists have figured out how dinosaurs lived. Some remarkable discoveries of fossilized skin provide information about how they looked.

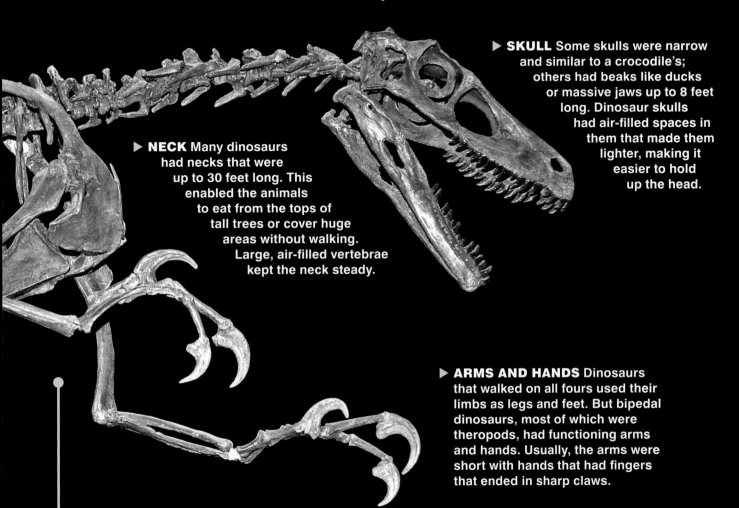

▶ **SKULL** Some skulls were narrow and similar to a crocodile's; others had beaks like ducks or massive jaws up to 8 feet long. Dinosaur skulls had air-filled spaces in them that made them lighter, making it easier to hold up the head.

▶ **NECK** Many dinosaurs had necks that were up to 30 feet long. This enabled the animals to eat from the tops of tall trees or cover huge areas without walking. Large, air-filled vertebrae kept the neck steady.

▶ **ARMS AND HANDS** Dinosaurs that walked on all fours used their limbs as legs and feet. But bipedal dinosaurs, most of which were theropods, had functioning arms and hands. Usually, the arms were short with hands that had fingers that ended in sharp claws.

FOSSIL EVIDENCE
Saurornitholestes (shown above) was a saurischian theropod, with birdlike feet and claws. It was bipedal and had short forelimbs. Its neck was average length and it had a long, flat jaw.

WORD

Vertebrae are small bones, connected to muscles, that in many animals and humans form a backbone. These animals, called vertebrates, also have vertebrae in their necks and tails. A **vertebra** is just one of these bones.

Open Wide

Different dinosaurs had teeth in different shapes and sizes. Some were sharp, others smooth, and still others were ridged or serrated. What do size, shape, and type of tooth tell us about a dinosaur? They let us know what kind of food the dinosaur ate.

WHAT TEETH TELL US

If a dinosaur had rounded, dull teeth, it probably used them to grind down on plants. If it had long, sharp teeth, like a lion's, then it probably used them to catch and eat other animals.

Camarasaurus, a plant eater, had rounded teeth.

Carcharodontosaurus, a meat eater, had sharp teeth.

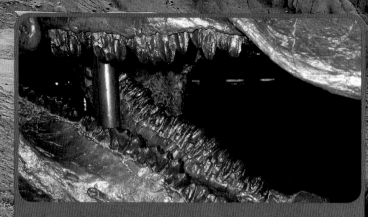

DID YOU KNOW?

Dinosaur teeth grew back if they broke or fell out. Sharks and crocodiles, modern descendants of the prehistoric creatures, can also grow new teeth.

CHEEKY CREATURES

Many plant-eating dinosaurs, such as *Styracosaurus* and *Triceratops* (above), had extra sets of teeth in their cheeks. These were used to grind the plants they ate into a mush that could be easily digested.

9"

▶ *Tyrannosaurus rex* had huge, banana-shaped teeth strong enough to bite into prey and crush bones without breaking or falling out.

8"

BONE UP!

Some dinosaurs didn't have any teeth at all— they had beaks. These toothless dinosaurs, including *Ornithomimus*, were prehistoric ancestors of today's birds.

7"

6"

▶ *Spinosaurus* had straight, sharp teeth in a narrow jaw to catch fish and smaller dinosaurs, similar to a modern crocodile.

5"

4"

▶ *Triceratops* had 400-800 teeth in multiple rows, giving it the serious chewing power it needed to eat lots of plant fiber.

▶ *Rebbachisaurus* looked big and fierce at 65 feet long. But due to its small head and serrated, arrow-shaped teeth, experts think it was a plant eater.

3"

▶ Small, birdlike *Troodon* had little, pointed, serrated teeth, suggesting that it ate both plants and meat.

2"

1"

Skin and Feathers

The soft parts of dinosaurs—skin, muscles, and tissue—became fossilized only very rarely, but some fossils have been discovered. Scientists combine what they learn from studying this fossil evidence with what they know about other animals to determine what dinosaurs may have looked like.

Edmontosaurus

Edmontosaurus skin fossil

Fossilized skin from the head of an *Edmontosaurus* was found by a team of Canadian scientists in 2013. They are examining this evidence under infrared light and heavy-duty microscopes to see if its color can be determined. Skin impressions, made when dinosaurs died on soft sand, also provide information about their skin.

Most large animals have skin that is shades of black, brown, green, or gray—colors that help animals camouflage themselves or regulate body temperatures by reflecting or absorbing heat. Scientists have made assumptions that dinosaur skin was similar, because that would have helped them survive.

DR. JOE SAYS

Birds and crocodiles, living relatives of dinosaurs, have very good color vision. Because of this, we assume that dinosaurs also saw colors, and may have used bright colors on their skin and feathers as a display to rivals and mates or to scare predators. Many dinosaurs may have sported crazy shades of blue, red, and yellow.

— *Dr. Joseph Sertich, Paleontologist*

EUREKA!

In 1999, high school student Tyler Lyson found a mummified *Edmontosaurus* skeleton, with skin attached, on a ranch in North Dakota. (Mummification is a process that dries and preserves skin; wind and sun can mummify a corpse under some conditions.) The mummified skin showed bumps rather than scales and suggested a striped pattern. Tyler now works at the Denver Museum of Nature & Science, studying turtle fossils.

Coelophysis

Ampelosaurus

Sinornithosaurus

BUMPS AND CREASES

Most scientists agree that dinosaur skin had bumps and creases. They have evidence of this from the Dakota fossil and from skin impressions.

SCALES

Scales are thin, separate pieces of tough tissue that cover the bodies of many animals in overlapping plates. Most reptiles have scales; skin impressions and a few fossils show dinosaurs had scales.

FEATHERS

Evidence—tiny bumps on bones where quills would attach and a few preserved feathers—proves that many dinosaurs were covered in feathers.

IN LIVING COLOR

Although most experts agree that dinosaur skin was mostly shades of black, brown, green, and gray, some parts of dinosaurs may have been brightly colored. Feathers first appeared on dinosaurs about 150 million years ago. Pretty feathers would have helped a dinosaur attract a mate, so there is a good reason why brightly feathered dinosaurs would have survived while others died out.

How can scientists figure out what colors dinosaur feathers were? They look at them under high-powered microscopes. By studying the shapes and concentrations of pigment molecules, which form colors, they know that some dinosaurs were striped in black, white, gray, or red, and some were iridescent.

Anchiornis

DINO DETAILS
44 JURASSIC THEROPODS

ALLOSAURS AND THEIR RELATIVES

	SIZE	AGE	FOSSILS	LOCATION
Aerosteon (air-oh-**STEE**-on)	L	LC		SA
Allosaurus (al-oh-**SORE**-us)	L	LJ		NA
Australovenator (oss-tra-loh-**VEN**-a-tore)	M	EC		AU
Chilantaisaurus (jee-lahn-tie-**SORE**-us)	S	EC		AS/EU
Concavenator (con-**CA**-ven-a-tore)	M	EC		EU
Fukuiraptor (foo-**KOO**-ee-rap-tore)	M	MC		AS
Megaraptor (**MEH**-guh-rap-tore)	L	MC		SA
Metriacanthosaurus (meh-tree-uh-**CAN**-thuh-sore-us)	L	LJ		EU
Monolophosaurus (**MAH**-no-loh-foe-sore-us)	M	LJ		AS
Neovenator (**NEE**-oh-ven-a-tore)	L	EC		EU
Orkoraptor (**OR**-koh-rap-tore)	L	LC		SA
Shidaisaurus (she-day-**SORE**-us)	L	MJ		AS
Siamotyrannus (see-**AM**-oh-tih-ran-us)	L	EC		AS
Siats (**SEE**-atch)	XL	MC		NA
Sinraptor dongi (sin-**RAP**-tore **DAHN**-yee)	L	LJ		AS
Sinraptor hepingensis (sin-**RAP**-tore heh-peen-**GEN**-sis)	L	LJ		AS
Yangchuanosaurus (**YANG**-shwan-oh-sore-us)	XL	LJ		AS

THE BIGGEST CARNIVORES

	SIZE	AGE	FOSSILS	LOCATION
Acrocanthosaurus (ak-roh-**CAN**-thuh-sore-us)	XL	EC		NA
Afrovenator (a-fro-**VEN**-a-tore)	L	EC		AF
Baryonyx (**BARE**-ee-ah-niks)	L	EC		EU/AF
Carcharodontosaurus (car-ca-roh-**DON**-tih-sore-us)	XL	LC		AF

	SIZE	AGE	FOSSILS	LOCATION
Condorraptor (**KON**-dor-rap-tore)	M	MJ		SA
Dubreuillosaurus (doo-**BROO**-ee-loh-sore-us)	L	MJ		EU
Duriavenator (dur-ee-ah-**VEN**-a-tore)	L	MJ		EU
Eocarcharia (ee-oh-car-**KEY**-a)	XL	EC		AF
Eustreptospondylus (you-**STREP**-toe-spon-duh-lus)	L	MJ		EU
Giganotosaurus (**JYE**-ga-no-tih-sore-us)	XXL	EC		SA
Ichthyovenator (ik-thee-oh-**VEN**-a-tore)	L	EC		AS
Irritator (**EAR**-uh-tay-tore)	L	MC		SA
Leshansaurus (leh-shan-**SORE**-us)	L	LJ		AS
Magnosaurus (mag-no-**SORE**-us)	M	MJ		EU
Mapusaurus (map-oo-**SORE**-us)	XXL	LC		EU
Marshosaurus (mar-sho-**SORE**-us)	M	LJ		NA
Megalosaurus (meg-a-loh-**SORE**-us)	L	MJ		EU
Oxalaia (ahks-a-**LIE**-a)	XL	LC		SA
Piatnitzkysaurus (py-a-**NEET**-skee-sore-us)	M	MJ		SA
Piveteausaurus (**PEE**-va-toe-sore-us)	XL	MJ		SA
Shaochilong (**SHAH**-chee-long)	L	EC		AS
Siamosaurus (si-am-oh-**SORE**-us)	L	EC		AS
Spinosaurus (**SPY**-no-sore-us)	XXL	LC		AF
Streptospondylus (**STREP**-toe-spon-duh-lus)	S	MJ		EU
Suchomimus (**SOOK**-oh-my-mus)	XL	EC		AF
Torvosaurus (**TORE**-voh-sore-us)	XL	LC		NA
Tyrannotitan (tie-**RA**-no-tie-tan)	XL	EC		SA

Baryonyx

LEGEND

Featured dinosaurs are set in red in the list above.

SIZE
XS	Under 5 feet
S	5-10 feet
M	10-20 feet
L	20-30 feet
XL	30-40 feet
XXL	Over 40 feet
UN	Unknown

AGE (years ago)
LT	Late Triassic (227-201 million)
EJ	Early Jurassic (201-180 million)
MJ	Middle Jurassic (180-159 million)
LJ	Late Jurassic (159-144 million)
EC	Early Cretaceous (144-98 million)
LC	Late Cretaceous (98-66 million)

FOSSILS
- Full skeleton
- Partial skeleton
- Skull
- Bone
- Teeth

LOCATION
AS	Asia
AF	Africa
EU	Europe
AU	Australia
NA	North America
SA	South America
AN	Antarctica

Jurassic Theropods
Big Meat Eaters

Monolophosaurus

After millions of years of evolution, dinosaurs had become bigger and deadlier. Slight changes in their bodies—sharper claws, stronger tails that helped with balance—had made them more efficient predators. Some of the most famous big meat eaters, such as *Allosaurus*, *Spinosaurus*, and *Carcharodontosaurus*, were the apex predators of their time. They were also among the biggest theropods that ever lived.

Big to Biggest Carnivores

By the Early Jurassic period, dinosaurs had spread to every continent. At that time, all the continents were joined in one landmass called Pangaea. The dinosaurs had no trouble getting from one continent to another, because there were no oceans separating them.

YANGCHUANOSAURUS

➡ A bipedal carnivore that feasted on large sauropods

➡ Named for location found, in Yangchuan, China

➡ Was 36 feet long; weighed 6,000 pounds

➡ Had ridges and knobs on its face

FUN FACT *Yangchuanosaurus* was discovered by a construction worker building a dam.

CARCHARODONTOSAURUS

➡ A bipedal carnivore with a massive body and tail

➡ Named for its teeth (*karkhar* means "jagged" and *odon* means "tooth" in Greek)

➡ Was 25–45 feet long; weighed up to 16,000 pounds

➡ Had sharp, 8-inch-long teeth and a 5-foot-long head

FUN FACT *Carcharodontosaurus* was larger than *Tyrannosaurus rex* but was more lightly constructed.

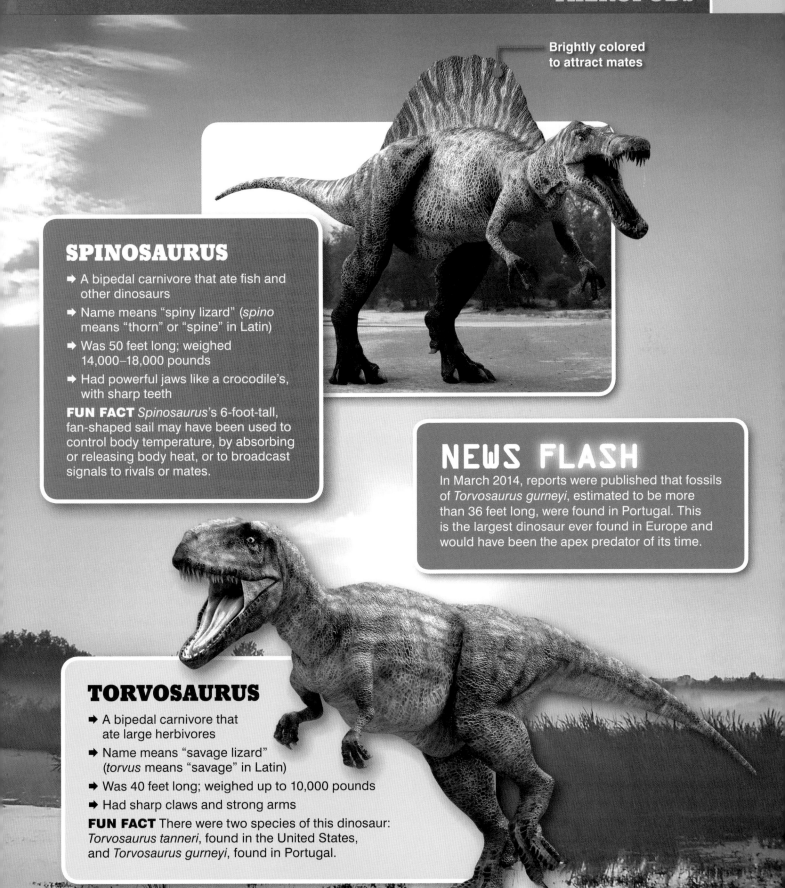

Brightly colored to attract mates

SPINOSAURUS

➡ A bipedal carnivore that ate fish and other dinosaurs

➡ Name means "spiny lizard" (*spino* means "thorn" or "spine" in Latin)

➡ Was 50 feet long; weighed 14,000–18,000 pounds

➡ Had powerful jaws like a crocodile's, with sharp teeth

FUN FACT *Spinosaurus*'s 6-foot-tall, fan-shaped sail may have been used to control body temperature, by absorbing or releasing body heat, or to broadcast signals to rivals or mates.

NEWS FLASH

In March 2014, reports were published that fossils of *Torvosaurus gurneyi*, estimated to be more than 36 feet long, were found in Portugal. This is the largest dinosaur ever found in Europe and would have been the apex predator of its time.

TORVOSAURUS

➡ A bipedal carnivore that ate large herbivores

➡ Name means "savage lizard" (*torvus* means "savage" in Latin)

➡ Was 40 feet long; weighed up to 10,000 pounds

➡ Had sharp claws and strong arms

FUN FACT There were two species of this dinosaur: *Torvosaurus tanneri*, found in the United States, and *Torvosaurus gurneyi*, found in Portugal.

Allosaurus: Different Lizard

What was different about *Allosaurus*? It had more vertebrae than some other dinosaurs—9 in its neck, 14 in its back, 5 near its hips—and ribs that gave it a barrel chest and a potbelly. It also had five teeth in the bones at the tip of its snout—most theropods had four.

With 70 supersharp teeth and 8-inch claws, this dinosaur occupied the top of the food chain. It also had the advantage of a jaw joint that made it able to open its mouth very wide to hold big chunks of meat.

Allosaurus is well known because more than 45 full skeletons have been found, many of them in Utah, Colorado, and Wyoming. Other fossils have been found in Europe and Tanzania.

PALEO DATA

ALLOSAURUS

PRONUNCIATION
al-*oh*-**SORE**-*us*

SIZE
28 feet long;
weighed 4,000-8,000 pounds

AGE
Late Jurassic (about
145 million years ago)

LOCATION
Western United States;
Europe; Africa

FOSSILS
Many complete skeletons

DIET
Meat

DID YOU KNOW?

More than 10,000 *Allosaurus* fossils have been found. There were at least three different species of this dinosaur.

COOL SHADES
Bony ridges over each eye may have served as sunshades.

FRIENDS OR FOES?

In many places, several *Allosaurus* fossils have been found together. There are two scientific theories about why this might be. Some experts think that they cooperated and hunted in packs. Others believe that they fought over the same prey, and sometimes even bit each other to get the best pieces to eat, which is why they were found together.

SAURUS STORY

"BIG AL"

When a team of paleontologists found a nearly complete *Allosaurus* skeleton in Wyoming in 1991, at first they thought it was an adult dinosaur. With further study, they realized that it was not fully grown and was probably an adolescent. The bones told the story of the difficult life this young dinosaur had led. It had lost limbs, broken ribs and other bones, and contracted infections before its early death. The scientists named the skeleton "Big Al" and wrote its life story. Later, a television show called *The Ballad of Big Al*, a re-creation of its life from birth to death, was produced.

Adapting for Survival

Evolution is the scientific theory about how living things change over time. As dinosaurs evolved, some were born with features that made them better able to survive and compete for food, water, territory, and mates. A dinosaur with a useful new feature survived and passed that feature on to its offspring. After thousands of years, dinosaurs with that feature were more successful, and dinosaurs without the useful feature died off.

STARTING WITH ARCHOSAURS

Reptiles called archosaurs dominated in the Early Triassic period, but many types of archosaurs became extinct by the Early Jurassic period. Two major groups evolved from archosaurs before they vanished: crocodiles and dinosaurs. The first crocodiles and the first dinosaurs were similar to each other. Then each group evolved to become better suited to its environment, and after a few hundred million years of evolution, they were very different from one another.

Archosaur

Protosuchus, *an early crocodile*

Eoraptor, *an early dinosaur*

Deinosuchus from the Late Cretaceous period:
▶ Larger than early crocodile; grew to 45 feet long
▶ Larger, stronger jaw

Antarctosaurus, from the Late Cretaceous period:
▶ Larger than early dinosaurs, grew to more than 100 feet long
▶ Developed a long neck to reach the tops of trees
▶ Ate plants, which were plentiful in its time

Species evolve over time, and successful species are the ones best able to thrive in their environments.

FANCY FEATURES

Some dinosaurs developed specialized features that helped them eat better or avoid attacks.

Therizinosaurus developed extralong claws with which it could rake trees and gather leaves and seeds to eat.

Ornithopods, such as *Iguanodon*, evolved a set of teeth that made them able to chew their food and get more nutrition from it.

Ankylosaurus evolved a set of plates on its body made of heavy bone, which helped protect it from attack.

Brachiosaurus developed long front limbs to elevate its long neck to eat from the treetops.

DINO DETECTIVE

PALEONTOLOGY KIT

Professional paleontologists keep a set of tools that help them do their work. Small rock hammers and pickaxes let them dig without harming fragile bones, brushes are used to remove dirt, and magnifying glasses help them take a closer look. One of the most important tools a scientist has is a notebook for recording information.

DINO DETAILS
66 FEATHERED THEROPODS

EARLY COMPSOGNATHUS

	SIZE	AGE	FOSSILS	LOCATION
Aniksosaurus (an-ik-so-**SORE**-us)	S	MC	Bone	SA
Aorun (**EYE**-oh-run)	XS	LJ	Partial skeleton / Bone	AS
Coelurus (see-**LUR**-us)	S	LJ	Partial skeleton	NA
Lourinhanosaurus (loh-reen-**YAH**-no-sore-us)	L	LJ	Partial skeleton	EU
Nedcolbertia (ned-kohl-**BARE**-tee-a)	S	EC	Partial skeleton	NA
Ornitholestes (or-nih-thoh-**LES**-teez)	S	LJ	Partial skeleton	NA
Phaedrolosaurus (fee-droh-loh-**SORE**-us)	UN	EC	Teeth	SA
Richardoestesia (ri-**KARD**-oh-es-**TEE**-zee-a)	S	LC	Teeth	NA
Sciurumimus (sy-ore-uh-**MY**-mus)	XS	LJ	Full skeleton	EU
Sinosauropteryx (sy-no-sore-**OP**-tur-iks)	XS	EC	Full skeleton	AS
Teinurosaurus (tie-**NOO**-roh-sore-us)	L	LJ	Bone	EU
Tugulusaurus (too-**GOO**-loo-sore-us)	L	EC	Bone	AS
Xinjiangovenator (sheen-jee-yong-oh-**VEN**-a-tore)	S	EC	Bone	AS
Zuolong (**ZOO**-long)	S	LJ	Skull	AS

COMPSOGNATHUS AND ITS RELATIVES

	SIZE	AGE	FOSSILS	LOCATION
Aristosuchus (a-ris-toe-**SOO**-kus)	S	EC	Bone	EU
Compsognathus (komp-sog-**NAY**-thus)	XS	LJ	Full skeleton	EU
Huaxiagnathus (hwax-ee-ag-**NAY**-thus)	S	EC	Partial skeleton	AS
Juravenator (joo-rah-**VEN**-a-tore)	XS	LJ	Full skeleton	EU
Mirischia (meer-**ISH**-ee-a)	S	EC	Bone	EU
Scipionyx (**SKIP**-ee-on-iks)	S	EC	Bone	EU
Sinocalliopteryx (sy-no-cal-ee-**OP**-tur-iks)	S	EC	Full skeleton	AS

TYRANT DINOSAURS

	SIZE	AGE	FOSSILS	LOCATION
Albertosaurus (al-**BUR**-toe-sore-us)	L	LC	Full skeleton	NA
Alioramus (al-ee-oh-**RAY**-mus)	M	LC	Partial skeleton	AF
Appalachiosaurus (ap-a-**LAY**-she-a-sore-us)	L	LC	Skull	NA
Aviatyrannis (**AY**-vee-a-tie-ran-iss)	XS	LJ	Bone	EU
Bagaraatan (**BAG**-uh-rah-tahn)	M	LC	Partial skeleton	AF
Bistahieversor (bis-tah-he-ee-**VUR**-sore)	M	LC	Partial skeleton	NA
Daspletosaurus (dah-**SPLEE**-toe-sore-us)	L	LC	Full skeleton	NA
Dilong (**DYE**-long)	S	EC	Full skeleton	AS
Dryptosaurus (drip-toe-**SORE**-us)	M	LC	Partial skeleton	NA
Eotyrannus (**EE**-oh-tie-ran-us)	M	EC	Partial skeleton	EU
Gorgosaurus (gore-go-**SORE**-us)	L	LC	Full skeleton	NA
Guanlong (**GWAN**-long)	S	LJ	Partial skeleton	AS
Iliosuchus (il-ee-o-**SOO**-cus)	S	MJ	Partial skeleton	EU
Juratyrant (**JOO**-rah-tie-rant)	S	LJ	Partial skeleton	EU
Kileskus (ky-**LES**-kus)	S	MJ	Bone	AS
Labocania (lah-boh-**KAY**-nee-a)	M	LC	Skull	NA
Lythronax (**LI**-throh-nax)	L	LC	Partial skeleton	NA
Nanotyrannus (na-noh-tie-**RAN**-us)	M	LC	Skull	NA
Nanuqsaurus (nah-nuke-**SORE**-us)	M	LC	Skull	NA
Proceratosaurus (pro-ser-a-toe-**SORE**-us)	S	MC	Partial skeleton	EU
Qianzhousaurus (key-an-shoo-**SORE**-us)	UN	LC	Skull	AS
Raptorex (rap-**TOR**-ex)	S	EC	Partial skeleton	AS
Sinotyrannus (sy-no-tie-**RAN**-us)	XL	EC	Partial skeleton	NA/AS
Stokesosaurus (**STOHKS**-uh-sore-us)	M	LJ	Partial skeleton / Partial skeleton	NA
Tarbosaurus (tar-bow-**SORE**-us)	L	LC	Full skeleton	AS
Teratophoneus (tair-a-toe-**FOE**-nee-us)	M	LC	Partial skeleton	NA
Tyrannosaurus (tie-**RAN**-oh-sore-us)	XL	LC	Full skeleton	NA/AF
Xiongguanlong (**SHEE**-yong-gwahn-long)	M	EC	Skull / Bone	AS
Yutyrannus (you-tie-**RAN**-us)	L	EC	Full skeleton	AS
Zhuchengtyrannus (zhoo-cheng-tie-**RAN**-us)	XL	LC	Skull	AS

OSTRICH MIMICS

	SIZE	AGE	FOSSILS	LOCATION
Anserimimus (**AN**-sair-ih-my-mus)	XS	LC	Partial skeleton	AF
Archaeornithomimus (ar-kee-or-nih-thoh-**MY**-mus)	M	LC	Full skeleton	AS
Beishanlong (**BAY**-shan-long)	M	EC	Partial skeleton	AS
Deinocheirus (dy-nuh-**KY**-rus)	M	LC	Bone	AF
Gallimimus (ga-lih-**MY**-mus)	M	LC	Full skeleton	AF
Garudimimus (ga-roo-duh-**MY**-mus)	M	LC	Skull / Bone	AF
Harpymimus (har-pee-**MY**-mus)	S	MC	Skull / Bone	AF
Hexing (hay-**ZHING**)	XS	EC	Bone	AS
Kinnareemimus (kih-nuh-ree-**MY**-mus)	XS	EC	Bone	AS
Nqwebasaurus (nih-kweh-buh-**SORE**-us)	XS	EC	Full skeleton	AF
Ornithomimus (or-nih-thoh-**MY**-mus)	M	LC	Full skeleton	NA/AF
Pelecanimimus (pel-uh-kan-uh-**MY**-mus)	S	EC	Skull	EU
Shenzhousaurus (shen-zhoo-**SORE**-us)	S	EC	Full skeleton	AS
Sinornithomimus (sy-nor-nih-thoh-**MY**-mus)	S	LC	Full skeleton	AS
Struthiomimus (strooth-ee-oh-**MY**-mus)	M	LC	Full skeleton	NA

LEGEND

Featured dinosaurs are set in red in the list above.

SIZE
- XS Under 5 feet
- S 5-10 feet
- M 10-20 feet
- L 20-30 feet
- XL 30-40 feet
- XXL Over 40 feet
- UN Unknown

AGE (years ago)
- LT Late Triassic (227-201 million)
- EJ Early Jurassic (201-180 million)
- MJ Middle Jurassic (180-159 million)
- LJ Late Jurassic (159-144 million)
- EC Early Cretaceous (144-98 million)
- LC Late Cretaceous (98-66 million)

FOSSILS
- Full skeleton
- Partial skeleton
- Skull
- Bone
- Teeth

LOCATION
- AS Asia
- AF Africa
- EU Europe
- AU Australia
- NA North America
- SA South America
- AN Antarctica

Feathered Theropods
Coelurosaurs, Including Tyrants and Ostrich Mimics

Tyrannosaurus rex

Coelurosaurs ("hollow-tailed lizards") were a diverse group. *Compsognathus*, which was about the size of a turkey, and 40-foot-long *Tyrannosaurus rex* were both coelurosaurs. Although the dinosaurs in this group looked different from one another, they all had stiff tails and feathers of some sort. They lived from the Late Jurassic period to the Late Cretaceous period; during that time, some of them (such as *T. rex*) became bigger and deadlier, while others (such as *Ornithomimus*) became more like birds.

Tyrants and Birds

Many kinds of tyrant dinosaurs lived at the end of the Cretaceous period in North America and Asia. A tyrant is a creature that uses power to control weaker creatures. Most of the tyrant dinosaurs were the biggest and strongest animals in their environment; they fought and ate some of the other animals in their habitats. They had massive skulls, sharp teeth, small arms, and big tails, which helped them balance. The biggest, most deadly of the tyrants is the famous *Tyrannosaurus rex*.

ALBERTOSAURUS

➡ A bipedal carnivore, related to *T. rex* but only half its size
➡ Named for the Canadian province of Alberta, where it ruled Earth 5 million years before *T. rex*
➡ Was 25 feet long; weighed about 4,000 pounds
➡ Had two fingers on each of its short arms

FUN FACT Bones of 26 of these dinosaurs were found at one site, suggesting *Albertosaurus* traveled in packs.

COMPSOGNATHUS

➡ A bipedal carnivore with scales covering its skin
➡ Named for its long, thin jaw (*kompsos* means "elegant" in Greek)
➡ Was 2–4 feet long; weighed about 6 pounds
➡ Had clawed hands good for catching and holding its prey

FUN FACT Fossilized tracks show that *Compsognathus* was fast enough to catch speedy lizards; a skeleton was found with lizard fossils in its stomach.

ORNITHOLESTES

➡ A bipedal carnivore, thought to be a fast runner

➡ Name means "bird robber" in Greek

➡ Was about 5–7 feet long; weighed about 25 pounds

➡ Had a long head and a crested snout

FUN FACT *Ornitholestes*'s long tail may have provided balance when it darted after small prey such as lizards.

TYRANT TEETH

Tyrant dinosaurs had lots of big, sharp teeth. As many as 70 teeth lined their jaws and gave them a frightening appearance. Their teeth had tiny cracks, but these cracks didn't make them weaker the way they do in human teeth. The cracks helped distribute pressure along the jaws. This meant that the tyrants could bite with tremendous force without breaking their teeth.

STRUTHIOMIMUS

➡ A bipedal carnivore that ate reptiles, mammals, and insects that could be swallowed whole

➡ Name means "ostrich mimic" in Greek

➡ Was about 15 feet long; weighed about 300 pounds

➡ Had a hard beak but no teeth

FUN FACT A long neck and tail balanced each other out, allowing *Struthiomimus*, considered one of the fastest dinosaurs, to speed along.

Rex means "king," and *Tyrannosaurus rex* was king of the dinosaurs, the ultimate apex predator. But that doesn't mean it had an easy or uncomplicated life. Fossils show that *T. rex* was gored by herbivores, lost limbs in fights, and was sometimes preyed upon by members of its own species. The fact that *T. rex* fossils are usually found individually suggests that they were **loners** and didn't hunt in packs.

It's a misconception that *Tyrannosaurus rex* had poor vision. It could see about ten times farther than humans can. Its deep set eye sockets and eyes pointed straight ahead, giving *T. rex* better depth perception (which helped it see things farther away) than those dinosaurs with eyes pointed to the sides.

FOSSIL FILE

Although it can't be proved, because there are no live specimens to test, scientists assume *T. rex* had the strongest bite of any animal that ever lived. They base this assumption on the size of its jaws and the way the jaws opened and closed.

BITE MIGHT

Bite strength is measured in pounds per square inch, or psi. Computer models show that *T. rex*'s bite strength was more than 12,600 psi. How does that compare with creatures alive today?

Human
About 200 psi

Siberian tiger
About 1,000 psi

PALEO DATA

TYRANNOSAURUS

PRONUNCIATION
*tie-**RAN**-oh-sore-us*

SIZE
40 feet long; weighed
10,000-15,000 pounds

AGE
Late Cretaceous,
about 65 million years ago

LOCATION
Western U.S. and Canada;
Mongolia

FOSSILS
Many complete skeletons

DIET
Meat

T. rex's puny forearms, which would not have been helpful in attacks, lead some scientists to think that *T. rex* was a scavenger rather than a hunter. Other scientists believe that these tiny arms were actually very strong and were used to grip live prey while the jaws worked on tearing flesh. Like many carnivores, *T. rex* was probably both a scavenger and a hunter.

Tasmanian devil
About 1,200 psi, the greatest
psi-to-body-weight ratio

Crocodile
3,700 psi, the highest
ever measured on testing
equipment

Great white shark
Estimated at 4,000 psi,
but never measured

A Dinosaur Named Sue

"Sue" is the nickname given to the best-preserved, most complete, and largest *Tyrannosaurus rex* skeleton ever discovered. Sue is more than 42 feet long and weighs 3,922 pounds. More than 90 percent of its bones were found, making it one of the most extraordinary dinosaur skeletons in the world.

Sue's skeleton was found in the badlands of South Dakota and now stands, reconstructed, in the Field Museum in Chicago. This remarkable find even includes the small forearms and the fragile bones of the inner ear, which are almost never found with *T. rex* skeletons. Since the exhibit opened in May 2000, more than 16 million people have visited Sue at the Field Museum, and paleontologists all over the world have studied it. So far, no one has determined whether Sue was male or female—the skeleton was named for the paleontologist who discovered it, Sue Hendrickson.

FOSSIL FILE

Although Sue's brain wasn't fossilized, its braincase (the part of the skull that holds the brain) was. By putting the braincase through a CT scanner, scientists were able to determine that a large part of Sue's brain was devoted to detecting smells.

CIRCLES OF LIFE

Scientists can estimate the age of a dinosaur by checking growth rings on its bones. Rings show the different rates of growth that occur during different times of life—slow in infancy, fast during the teenage years, very little during adulthood. Sue is estimated to be 28 years old, making it the oldest *T. rex* ever studied.

EUREKA!

Sue may never have been found if not for a flat tire. Several researchers were ready to drive home from a field trip in the badlands when their car got a flat. Most of the group went to a nearby town to have the tire repaired, but Sue Hendrickson decided to stay behind and look around a field site that the group hadn't explored. Walking around the base of a cliff, she looked up and saw a few bones nestled in the rocks about 8 feet above her head. The bones were big enough to excite her, and later, when the entire extraordinary skeleton was finally uncovered, it was named for her.

Eyes and Vision

fossils of dinosaurs' eyeballs have ever been discovered. Scientists can evaluate a dinosaur's field of
vision—how much it could see at any given moment in time—and the sharpness of its eyesight by examining
the placement of the eyes in the skull and the size of the eye sockets. Experts can also determine how well a
dinosaur saw in the dark.

EYES FRONT, EYES ON THE SIDE

Some carnivores had eyes in front of the head; this gave them binocular vision (*bi* means "two" in Latin; *ocular* means "eye"). Their eyes worked together to produce one image, and that image would have been fairly sharp. Binocular vision also allowed for good depth perception—telling how far away an object is.

Most herbivores had eyes on the sides of their head. Each eye worked on its own and produced a separate image. This gave a wider range of vision—they could see predators coming from more directions—but the images were not as sharp as with binocular vision.

▶ *Stegosaurus* had two small eyes on its small head. Its vision was probably poor compared to other dinosaurs. *Stegosaurus* probably used its sense of smell to find food and detect predators, and kept its head low as it browsed the ground.

NIGHT VISION?

Did dinosaurs see in the dark? Scientific studies on light-sensitive proteins and rings of bones around dinosaur eyes support the idea that some dinosaurs had night vision.

▶ *Apatosaurus* had small eyes on the sides of its relatively small head. Its vision was probably not as acute as other dinosaurs. But being huge kept *Apatosaurus* safe from predators, so it did not need to see well.

Like all animals, dinosaurs used their senses and intelligence to interpret the world and survive in it. Each group of dinosaurs developed the senses needed for the way it lived.

▶ *Limaysaurus* eyes were large compared to the size of its head. This may have enhanced its sight. *Limaysaurus* was an herbivore and a sauropod, but it was not gigantic like some other sauropods. Good eyesight would have helped it avoid predators.

▶ *Velociraptor* had eyes on the sides of its head. The position of its eyes as part of its narrow jaw gave it a very wide field of vision.

▶ *T. rex* eyes faced front, much like human eyes— but the dinosaur had much bigger eyes than a human's, so its vision was much sharper than ours.

▶ *Triceratops* eyes were on the sides of the head, so it could see predators coming from the side as well as the front and back.

Dinosaurs used their senses of hearing and smell to find food and avoid predators. Their intelligence—higher in some groups than in others—also helped them survive. The scene on the right describes how a dinosaur might have used its senses to become aware of—and escape—a predator.

HEARING

After studying inner ears in dinosaur skulls and comparing them to those of living animals, scientists concluded that dinosaurs could have heard low-frequency sounds fairly well. This meant they would have been able to hear the sounds made by other dinosaurs, rain falling, and thunder crashing. They probably could not have heard high-pitched sounds, such as those made by birds.

Soft tissue didn't fossilize well, so there is no evidence that dinosaurs had ears on the outside of their skulls. Since birds—living relatives of dinosaurs—don't have ears, dinosaurs probably didn't either.

LEARN THE BASICS

Learning about rocks and fossils is one of the first steps to becoming a dinosaur detective. Paleontologists study for many years to understand the geologic features—especially soil and rocks—where dinosaurs bones are found. They become familiar with many kinds of bones, tracks, coprolites, and other traces of dinosaur life. When paleontologists see a bone sticking out of the ground or just beneath the surface, they can determine if it's a fossil. Much of what we know about dinosaurs comes from studying fossils or fossilized impressions, so learning about them is very important.

COMMUNICATION

No one knows for sure if dinosaurs could communicate. Like modern animals, they had the equipment to make sounds such as roars, bellows, squeaks, grunts, and grumbles. Some head crests were extensions of breathing apparatuses and may have amplified sound. Feathers, head attachments, and wings could also have been used to make motions directed to one another, the way modern birds and other animals do.

OLFACTION

Olfaction—the sense of smell—was an important sense for dinosaurs; whether their food source was plants or meat, they recognized it by its scent. Studies of dinosaur skulls have shown enlarged olfactory (smell) organs—for example, more than half of T. rex's brain was connected to its sense of smell.

ON THE SCENE

The ground is wet and cold against its feet as *Parasaurolophus* runs through the dark forest. Its field of vision is narrow and its eyes are not particularly large, so the small carnivore lurking behind a tree goes unnoticed, but it hears the rustling of the branches and senses danger. The next hint of a predator comes through the nose; an odor of dried blood and rotted meat wafts through the air. Finally, it sees a small *Deinonychus* coming toward it, sharp claws extended. But *Parasaurolophus* has a head start; it rises to a two-legged posture and runs as fast as it can.

INTELLIGENCE

Scientists have a way of estimating how smart dinosaurs were; it's called the encephalization quotient, or EQ. An estimate is made of a dinosaur's body size and brain size. Brain size is estimated based on the size of the skull's braincase—the bigger the braincase, the bigger the brain that could fit into it. Body size is compared to the brain size to get the EQ. No one can say that EQ is a true measure of intelligence—but we do know that human beings have the biggest brains of all animals compared to our body size, and we're also the most intellectually advanced animals.

Which were the smartest dinosaurs? *Troodon* had an EQ of almost 6, the highest. Big sauropods such as *Argentinosaurus* had the lowest EQs, barely 0.1.

Argentinosaurus

Troodon

ALVAREZSAURUS AND ITS RELATIVES

	SIZE	AGE	FOSSILS	LOCATION
Achillesaurus (a-kill-ee-**SORE**-us)	S	LC	Bone	SA
Albertonykus (al-bur-toe-**NY**-kus)	XS	LC	Bone	NA
Albinykus (al-bee-**NY**-kus)	XS	LC	Bone	AS
Alnashetri (al-nuh-**SHEH**-tree)	S	LC	Bone	SA
Alvarezsaurus (al-vuh-rez-**SORE**-us)	S	LC	Bone	SA
Bonapatenykus (boh-nuh-par-tuh-**NY**-kus)	S	LC	Bone	SA
Bradycneme (**BRAY**-dee-kuh-neem)	S	LC	Bone	EU
Ceratonykus (sehr-uh-toe-**NY**-kus)	S	LC	Partial skeleton	AS
Haplocheirus (hap-loh-**CARE**-us)	S	LJ	Partial skeleton	AS
Kol (**COHL**)	S	LC	Bone	AS
Linhenykus (lin-huh-**NY**-kus)	XS	LC	Partial skeleton	AS
Mononykus (mah-no-**NY**-kus)	XS	LC	Partial skeleton	AS
Parvicursor (par-vi-**KUHR**-sore)	XS	LC	Bone	AS
Patagonykus (pa-tuh-go-**NY**-kus)	S	LC	Partial skeleton	SA
Pedopenna (peh-doh-**PEH**-nah)	XS	LJ	Bone	AS
Shuvuuia (shoo-**VOO**-ee-a)	XS	LC	Skull, Partial skeleton	AS
Xixianykus (shee-shee-uh-**NY**-kus)	XS	LC	Partial skeleton	AS
Yixianosaurus (yee-shee-a-noh-**SORE**-us)	XS	EC	Partial skeleton	AS

THERIZINOSAURUS, SEGNOSAURUS, AND THEIR RELATIVES

	SIZE	AGE	FOSSILS	LOCATION
Alxasaurus (awl-shah-**SORE**-us)	M	EC	Partial skeleton	AS
Beipiaosaurus (bay-pee-ow-**SORE**-us)	S	EC	Partial skeleton	AS
Enigmosaurus (eh-nihg-moh-**SORE**-us)	M	LC	Partial skeleton	AS
Erliansaurus (er-lee-on-**SORE**-us)	S	LC	Partial skeleton	AS
Erlikosaurus (er-lik-oh-**SORE**-us)	M	LC	Teeth, Skull	AS
Falcarius (fal-**CARE**-ee-us)	M	EC	Full skeleton	NA

	SIZE	AGE	FOSSILS	LOCATION
Jianchangosaurus (jee-en-chan-goh-**SORE**-us)	S	EC	Full skeleton	AS
Nanshiungosaurus (nan-**SHUN**-goh-sore-us)	L	EC	Bone	AS
Neimongosaurus (neh-ee-mon-goh-**SORE**-us)	S	LC	Full, Partial skeleton	AS
Nothronychus (nah-throh-**NY**-kus)	M	EC	Partial skeleton	NA
Segnosaurus (**SEG**-noh-sore-us)	M	LC	Partial skeleton	AS
Suzhousaurus (**SOO**-joe-sore-us)	M	EC	Partial skeleton	AS
Therizinosaurus (theh-rih-**ZEE**-noh-sore-us)	XL	LC	Bone	AS

OVIRAPTOR AND ITS RELATIVES

	SIZE	AGE	FOSSILS	LOCATION
Ajancingenia (ah-han-**CHIN**-hen-ee-uh)	M	LC	Partial skeleton	AS
Anzu (**AHN**-zoo)	M	LC	Partial skeleton	NA
Avimimus (ah-vee-**MY**-mus)	S	LC	Partial skeleton	AS
Caudipteryx (caw-**DIP**-tur-iks)	XS	EC	Full skeleton	AS
Chirostenotes (**KY**-roh-sten-oh-teez)	S	LC	Partial skeleton	NA
Citipati (**CHI**-tih-puh-tee)	S	LC	Full skeleton	AS
Choncoraptor (**KON**-koh-rap-tore)	S	LC	Partial skeleton	AS
Elmisaurus (el-mee-**SORE**-us)	S	LC	Bone	AS
Hagryphus (**HAH**-gree-fus)	S	LC	Bone	NA
Heyuannia (**HAY**-yoo-on-ee-a)	S	LC	Bone	AS
Incisivosaurus (in-**SY**-zih-voh-sore-us)	XS	EC	Skull, Partial skeleton	AS
Khaan (**KAHN**)	XS	LC	Full skeleton	AS
Microvenator (my-croh-ven-**A**-tore)	XS	EC	Partial skeleton	NA
Oviraptor (**OH**-vih-rap-tore)	S	LC	Full skeleton	AS
Protarchaeopteryx (proh-tahr-kee-**OP**-tur-iks)	XS	EC	Partial skeleton	AS
Rinchenia (rin-cheh-**NEE**-a)	S	LC	Skull, Bone	AS

LEGEND

Featured dinosaurs are set in red in the list above.

SIZE
- XS Under 5 feet
- S 5-10 feet
- M 10-20 feet
- L 20-30 feet
- XL 30-40 feet
- XXL Over 40 feet
- UN Unknown

AGE (years ago)
- LT Late Triassic (227-201 million)
- EJ Early Jurassic (201-180 million)
- MJ Middle Jurassic (180-159 million)
- LJ Late Jurassic (159-144 million)
- EC Early Cretaceous (144-98 million)
- LC Late Cretaceous (98-66 million)

FOSSILS
- Full skeleton
- Partial skeleton
- Skull
- Bone
- Teeth

LOCATION
- AS Asia
- AF Africa
- EU Europe
- AU Australia
- NA North America
- SA South America
- AN Antarctica

Near-Raptors Theropods

Caudipteryx

Near-raptors looked a lot like birds. These dinosaurs' arms were similar to wings and covered with feathers. Many near-raptors ate plants, which they probably chopped off with their claws and beaked jaws. Closely related to birds of prey, which are called raptors, most near-raptors were less than 10 feet tall. *Therizinosaurus*, however, was an exception—at almost 40 feet long, it was one of the biggest theropods. Many of these creatures, such as *Oviraptor*, were found in Asia, and some have been found in North and South America.

Small and Fast

This group of small, fast birdlike theropods from the Late Cretaceous period have been confusing scientists for decades because they are hard to classify. At first it was assumed that they were raptors, but their hands and claws are not quite right for that group. Some think they are related to ostrich mimics, but they have differences from that group as well. They probably had very large chests, like birds, and were covered with feathers. They have been found in South America and Asia.

SHUVUUIA

➡ A bipedal carnivore that was a fast runner
➡ Named for the Mongolian word for "bird," *shuvuu*
➡ Was about 3 feet long; weighed 6 pounds
➡ Was small and birdlike, with a long, sharp beak

FUN FACT Experts think *Shuvuuia* was covered with feathers.

THERIZINOSAURUS

➡ A bipedal herbivore, possibly also an insectivore
➡ Named for its long claws (*therizo* means "scythe," a sharp, curved cutting tool, in Greek)
➡ Was about 30 feet long; weighed up to 6,000 pounds
➡ Had claws about 2 feet long, the length of a human arm—longer than the claws of any other animal that has ever lived

FUN FACT Few *Therizinosaurus* fossils have ever been found; it was initially thought to be a turtle.

MONONYKUS

➤ A bipedal carnivore that ate ants and other insects

➤ Name means "single claw" in Greek

➤ Was about 3 feet long; weighed about 10 pounds

➤ Had large eyes, thought to give it good night vision for hunting in the cool evenings of its desert habitat

FUN FACT *Mononykus* had one claw at the end of each arm, which it may have used to dig insects out of the ground.

NEWS FLASH

In March 2014, scientists made official a new near-raptor discovery. Named *Anzu,* after a feathered demon in Sumerian mythology, it was almost 11 feet long, weighed 600 pounds, and had a huge beak and a few razor-sharp teeth. Fossils of this fierce beast were found in three different areas of the Hell Creek rock formation in North and South Dakota. Nicknamed "the chicken from hell" based on its shape—like a giant, elongated chicken—and area it was discovered, it is the most complete oviraptorosaur skeleton found in North America.

SEGNOSAURUS

➤ A bipedal herbivore, possibly an omnivore, with wide hips and a long neck

➤ Name means "slow lizard" in Latin

➤ Was about 15–30 feet long; weighed up to 4,000 pounds

➤ Had three fingers on each hand and four weight-bearing toes on each foot

FUN FACT *Segnosaurus* has features of ornithischians and prosauropods but it's a therizinosaur theropod.

Oviraptor: The Egg Thief?

This birdlike, flightless dinosaur looked very much like an ostrich, another bird that never flew. Like the ostrich, *Oviraptor* probably ran very fast, up to 40 miles per hour. Although it had no teeth, its sharp beak could crush small mammals and reptiles, and its sharp claws could capture and hold live prey.

? DID YOU KNOW?

Hard kicks from its long, strong legs and sharp pecks from its wide beak helped *Oviraptor* kill its prey.

DANCING DINOS

Oviraptor had arm fans, head crests, and tail feathers that may have been used to put on mating displays. This behavior is seen in birds today, in mating rituals that include dancing and shaking their tail feathers.

Snowy egret

PALEO DATA

OVIRAPTOR

PRONUNCIATION
OH-vih-rap-tore

SIZE
7 feet long; weighed about 65 pounds

AGE
Late Cretaceous period, about 70 million years ago

LOCATION
Mongolia; China

FOSSILS
Several complete skeletons

DIET
Meat, possibly also plants

SAURUS STORY

AN UNJUST ACCUSATION

Oviraptor means "egg thief." It got the name after its fossils were found on top of some broken eggs. Scientists thought that the eggs, which had no baby bones in them, had belonged to *Protoceratops*, and that *Oviraptor* had stolen the eggs and eaten the growing babies. Then, in 1993, an *Oviraptor* skeleton was found in brooding position on top of a nest full of eggs. These eggs did have fossilized babies in them—they were *Oviraptor* babies. From this discovery, scientists learned that *Oviraptor* did not steal and destroy eggs belonging to other dinosaurs. It was a good parent that cared for its young.

What's on the Menu?

About one-eighth of all dinosaurs were carnivores (meat eaters); they ate small mammals, reptiles, and other dinosaurs. The rest were herbivores and ate plants. Since the plant eaters were eaten by the meat eaters, the fact that there were more herbivores meant there was enough food for the carnivores. If there had been more meat eaters than plant eaters, the meat eaters would have used up their food source. Some dinosaurs were omnivores (*omni* means "all") and ate both meat and plants.

HERBIVORES AT THE ALL-DAY BUFFET

Plants have very few calories, which are the units of energy in food. In order to get enough energy to keep their big bodies nourished, plant eaters had to spend most of their time eating. Evergreen trees, ferns, and cycads—plants that look like palm trees but that have seed cones similar to fir trees—grew during the early years of the Age of Dinosaurs. By the end of the age, there were flowering plants for herbivores to eat, also.

Scansoriopteryx

OMNIVORES

Some dinosaurs, including *Scansoriopteryx*, were not choosy about their food. They ate everything—small reptiles and mammals, insects, seeds, fish, and plants.

Edmontosaurus

Dinosaurs chose a variety of types of nourishment and digested their food in a variety of ways.

WHAT DID CARNIVORES EAT?

A common belief about carnivorous dinosaurs is that they were constantly ripping big dinosaurs apart and eating them. It is true that carnivores attacked big herbivores, and even other carnivores. Some even preyed on their own species. But dinosaurs also ate small mammals, birds, and reptiles; fossilized remains of small creatures have been found in the rib cages of meat-eating dinosaurs.

Predators also ate young or sick and weak dinosaurs of other species. Finding and killing a big dinosaur, such as *Triceratops*, could keep *T. rex* nourished for several weeks—but eating a few small ones could do the same job with less effort and less danger.

Troodon

PISCIVORES

Some dinosaurs' diet consisted mainly of fish. Scientists classified these dinosaurs as piscivores. *Piscis* means "fish" in Latin.

Suchomimus

Feeding and Digesting

Different dinosaurs had different diets and ways of eating. Most dinosaur teeth and jaws were not designed for chewing. Carnivores ripped off chunks of meat and swallowed it, or downed small animals whole. Herbivore teeth stripped leaves off bark and swallowed them. The process of breaking down food was done in the stomach, not by the teeth.

SMALL MEAT MEALS

Most carnivores did not have to eat as much or as often as herbivores did, because meat is packed with calories from protein and fat. Carnivore digestion systems were fairly simple—a hunk of flesh or even a whole leg could be ripped off and swallowed without chewing. The food was broken down in the stomach, the protein was turned into energy, and the fat was stored for later.

SCAVENGERS OR PREDATORS?

Deinonychus and other raptors were vicious predators, meaning that they hunted live prey; dinosaur fossils with theropod teeth marks all over them have been found. But many big dinosaurs probably found a lot of their food by scavenging—looking for animals that were already dead and eating the remains.

A SIDE ORDER OF ROCKS

Some plant eaters found a way to help their digestive systems break down woody or tough plants: They swallowed small rocks, which mashed up food in their stomachs every time they moved. A few dinosaur skeletons have been found with these rocks, which are called gastroliths (*gastro* means "stomach," *lith* means "stone" in Greek), in their stomachs.

Gastroliths became smooth and shiny after grinding food. Some people collect these stones.

DR. JOE SAYS

Although many dinosaurs didn't chew, some advanced herbivores, including hadrosaurs and ceratopsids, developed the process of chewing to replace gastroliths. These dinosaurs did chew their food before swallowing it.
— *Dr. Joseph Sertich, Paleontologist*

BIG BELLIES

Large herbivores needed huge stomachs to hold and break down all the plants they had to eat to survive. Experts think that most herbivorous dinosaurs, such as *Brachiosaurus*, had fermentation chambers in their stomachs where stomach acids processed food so its nutrients could be absorbed.

Brachiosaurus

DINO DETAILS
63 PARAVIANS THEROPODS

DROMAEOSAURS

Name	Size	Age	Fossils	Location
Achillobator (a-kil-oh-**BAY**-tore)	M	LC	Partial skeleton	AS
Adasaurus (ay-duh-**SORE**-us)	S	LC	Partial skeleton	AS
Atrociraptor (a-**TROH**-sih-rap-tore)	XS	LC	Teeth	NA
Austroraptor (**OSS**-troh-rap-tore)	M	LC	Partial skeleton	AS
Balaur (**BAH**-lore)	XS	LC	Partial skeleton	EU
Bambiraptor (**BAM**-be-rap-tore)	XS	LC	Skull	NA
Buitreraptor (**BWEE**-tree-rap-tore)	XS	LC	Partial skeleton	SA
Cryptovolans (krip-toe-**VUL**-ans)	XS	EC	Partial skeleton	AS
Deinonychus (dy-**NAH**-nih-kus)	S	EC	Partial skeleton	NA
Dromaeosaurus (**DROH**-mee-oh-sore-us)	S	LC	Partial skeleton	NA
Epidexipteryx (eh-pih-deks-**IP**-tur-iks)	XS	LJ	Partial skeleton	AS
Graciliraptor (**GRA**-sil-ih-rap-tore)	XS	EC	Teeth, Partial skeleton	AS
Hesperonychus (hes-**PER**-ah-nih-kus)	XS	LC	Skull	NA
Itemirus (eye-tih-**MY**-rus)	S	LC	Skull	AS
Linheraptor (**LIN**-huh-rap-tore)	S	LC	Partial skeleton	AS
Luanchuanraptor (loo-un-**CHOO**-un-rap-tore)	S	LC	Partial skeleton	AS
Mahakala (mah-hah-kah-lah)	XS	LC	Partial skeleton	AS
Microraptor (**MY**-croh-rap-tore)	XS	EC	Partial skeleton	AS
Neuquenraptor (**NOO**-kwen-rap-tore)	S	LC	Bone	SA
Nuthetes (**NOO**-theh-teez)	S	EC	Teeth	EU
Ornithodesmus (or-nih-thoh-**DES**-mus)	S	EC	Bone	EU
Pamparaptor (**PAM**-puh-rap-tore)	S	LC	Bone	SA
Pyroraptor (**PY**-roh-rap-tore)	S	LC	Skull, Bone	EU
Rahonavis (rah-hoo-**NAY**-vis)	XS	LC	Partial skeleton	AF
Saurornitholestes (sore-or-nih-thoh-**LES**-teez)	S	LC	Partial skeleton	NA
Scansoriopteryx (skan-sore-ee-**OP**-tur-iks)	XS	EC	Partial skeleton	AS
Shanag (**SHAH**-nag)	S	EC	Bone	AF
Sinornithosaurus (**SY**-nor-nih-thoh-sore-us)	S	EC	Partial skeleton	AS
Tianyuraptor (tee-ahn-you-**RAP**-tore)	S	LJ	Partial skeleton	AS
Tsaagan (**SAH**-gan)	S	LC	Skull, Bone	AS
Unenlagia (oo-nen-**LAH**-ghee-a)	S	LC	Bone	SA
Unquillosaurus (oon-kee-oh-**SORE**-us)	S	LC	Bone	SA

Name	Size	Age	Fossils	Location
Utahraptor (**YOO**-tah-rap-tore)	M	EC	Partial skeleton	NA
Velociraptor (vuh-**LAH**-si-rap-tore)	S	LC	Partial skeleton	AS
Yurgovuchia (yuhr-go-voo-**chee**-a)	XS	EC	Bone	NA

TROODON AND ITS RELATIVES

Name	Size	Age	Fossils	Location
Archaeornithoides (ar-kee-**OR**-nih-thoy-deez)	XS	LC	Skull	AS
Borogovia (bo-roh-**GOH**-vee-a)	S	LC	Bone	AS
Byronosaurus (by-run-oh-**SORE**-us)	S	LC	Partial skeleton	AS
Geminiraptor (**JEH**-mih-ny-rap-tore)	S	EC	Bone	NA
Gobivenator (goh-bee-ven-**A**-tore)	XS	LC	Partial skeleton	AS
Koparion (koh-**PAR**-ee-on)	XS	LJ	Teeth	NA
Linhevenator (lin-heh-ven-**A**-tore)	XS	LC	Partial skeleton	AS
Mei (**MAY**)	XS	EC	Partial skeleton	AS
Pectinodon (pek-**TIH**-noh-don)	S	LC	Teeth	NA
Philovenator (fie-loh-ven-**A**-tore)	XS	LC	Partial skeleton	AS
Saurornithoides (sore-or-nih-**THOY**-deez)	S	LC	Skull	AS
Sinornithoides (sy-nor-nih-**THOY**-deez)	XS	LC	Partial skeleton	AS
Sinusonasus (sy-nyoo-**SO**-nay-sus)	XS	EC	Partial skeleton	AS
Talos (**TAY**-los)	S	LC	Partial skeleton	NA
Tochisaurus (**TOHK**-ih-sore-us)	S	LC	Bone	AS
Troodon (**TROH**-uh-don)	S	LC	Partial skeleton	NA
Urbacodon (uhr-**BAK**-uh-don)	XS	LC	Teeth	AS
Xiaotingia (shyow-**TIN**-gee-a)	XS	LJ	Partial skeleton	AS
Xixiasaurus (zee-zee-uh-**SORE**-us)	S	LC	Partial skeleton	AS
Zanabazar (zah-nuh-buh-**zar**)	S	LC	Skull, Partial skeleton	AS

AVIALAE

Name	Size	Age	Fossils	Location
Anchiornis (ahng-kee-**OR**-nis)	S	LJ	Skull	AS
Archaeopteryx (ar-kee-**OP**-tur-iks)	XS	LJ	Partial skeleton	EU
Gobipteryx (**GO**-bee-puh-tur-iks)	S	LC	Skull, Partial skeleton	AS
Hesperornis (hes-purr-**OR**-nis)	S	LC	Partial skeleton	NA
Ichthyornis (ick-theeh-**OR**-nis)	XS	LC	Teeth, Partial skeleton	NA
Protopteryx (pro-**top**-tur-iks)	XS	EC	Partial skeleton	AS
Vegavis (**VAY**-gah-vis)	XS	LC	Bone	AN
Vorona (**VORE**-oh-na)	S	LC	Bone	AF

LEGEND

Featured dinosaurs are set in red in the list above.

SIZE
- XS — Under 5 feet
- S — 5-10 feet
- M — 10-20 feet
- L — 20-30 feet
- XL — 30-40 feet
- XXL — Over 40 feet
- UN — Unknown

AGE (years ago)
- LT — Late Triassic (227-201 million)
- EJ — Early Jurassic (201-180 million)
- MJ — Middle Jurassic (180-159 million)
- LJ — Late Jurassic (159-144 million)
- EC — Early Cretaceous (144-98 million)
- LC — Late Cretaceous (98-66 million)

FOSSILS
- Full skeleton
- Partial skeleton
- Skull
- Bone
- Teeth

LOCATION
- AS — Asia
- AF — Africa
- EU — Europe
- AU — Australia
- NA — North America
- SA — South America
- AN — Antarctica

Paravians
Theropods

Were they birds or dinosaurs? Or were they both birds *and* dinosaurs? Paleontologists agree that all birds are descended from theropod dinosaurs. At some point, some dinosaurs had developed enough bird features to be considered avian (bird) dinosaurs. The dinosaurs in this section, the paravians, included some dinosaurs that were on the boundary between avian and non-avian dinosaurs, and some that were definitely birds. It also included *Troodon* and its family, a group of small, intelligent, vicious carnivores.

Pyroraptor

For the Birds

BAMBIRAPTOR

➡ A bipedal carnivore with sharp teeth and lethal claws

➡ Named based on its small size—either for the movie character Bambi, or, according to some, for the juvenile fossil found (*bambino* means "baby" in Italian)

➡ Was about 3 feet long; weighed 4–5 pounds

➡ Could fold its arms, the way modern birds tuck their wings

FUN FACT *Bambiraptor* was discovered by 14-year-old Wes Linster, who was fossil hunting with his family in Montana's Glacier National Park.

DROMAEOSAURUS

➡ A bipedal carnivore that was small and speedy

➡ Name means "running lizard" in Greek

➡ Was about 6 feet long; weighed up to 100 pounds

➡ Had a big, wide mouth and a stronger bite than other raptors of its time

FUN FACT Experts debate the purpose of the single big claw on each back foot. Some say it was used as a weapon, others say it was used to grip prey, and still others think it helped *Dromaeosaurus* climb trees.

HESPERORNIS

➡ A bipedal piscivore that was an excellent swimmer and diver

➡ Name means "western bird" in Greek

➡ Was about 6 feet long; weighed about 30 pounds

➡ Was unable to fly or walk well on land

FUN FACT *Hesperornis*'s movement is often compared to that of modern loons, but unlike modern birds, *Hesperornis* had small teeth lining its beak.

DEINONYCHUS

➡ A bipedal carnivore, thought to be a very fast runner

➡ Name means "terrible claw" in Greek

➡ Was about 10 feet long; weighed about 160 pounds

➡ Had a long, sharp, curved claw on the second toe of each foot, used for slashing and tearing apart prey

FUN FACT *Deinonychus* was one of the smartest dinosaurs, based on the size of its brain (relative to its body size), and may have adopted a pack approach to hunting.

▷ Supersharp claws on the hands and back legs were the main weapons *Deinonychus* used to make deep stab wounds and then rip apart prey.

Velociraptor: Speedy Thief

Velociraptor had long forearms, with sharp claws that it could pull in and push out as needed. When its claws weren't in use, it kept its arms tucked in, like a bird does with its wings. *Velociraptor* used its claws to catch prey and hold it while eating.

FOSSIL FILE

Though not a particularly fast runner, *Velociraptor* was an excellent jumper. It had hard, inflexible bones in its tail that helped it balance; this allowed it to jump as high as 10 feet straight up.

FACT OR FICTION?

Velociraptor is one of the most recognized dinosaurs, in part because it was featured in the movie *Jurassic Park*. In the movie, *Velociraptor* was a large, vicious, smart dinosaur that joined with others in a pack to attack big herbivores. In fact, it was not particularly large, vicious, or smart. The characteristics the movie gave to *Velociraptor* actually belonged to *Deinonychus*, a much larger and fiercer dinosaur.

▶ *Velociraptor* fossils show that their forearms had knobs that could have held feathers, and experts believe its feathers were probably used to attract mates and regulate body temperature.

PALEO DATA

VELOCIRAPTOR

PRONUNCIATION
vuh-**LAH**-*si*-rap-*tore*

SIZE
7 feet long; weighed 15–30 pounds

AGE
Late Cretaceous, about 80 million years ago

LOCATION
Mongolia

FOSSILS
Several complete skeletons

DIET
Meat

Was *Archaeopteryx* a bird or a dinosaur? Paleontologists have been debating this point since this small, ravenlike animal was discovered in a fossil bed in Germany in 1861. Some scientists say that it was a transitional animal between dinosaurs and birds; others consider *Archaeopteryx* to be the first bird.

PALEO DATA

ARCHAEOPTERYX

PRONUNCIATION
ar-*kee*-**OP**-*tur-iks*

SIZE
Under 2 feet long; weighed 1-2 pounds

AGE
Late Jurassic, about 145 million years ago

LOCATION
Germany

FOSSILS
Several complete skeletons

DIET
Meat

FLYING AND GLIDING

Although *Archaeopteryx* was covered with feathers, the feathers were not spaced properly for strong, fast flight. So while it could fly, it probably did more gliding than flying.

SIMILARITIES AND DIFFERENCES

Some characteristics *Archaeopteryx* shared with dinosaurs:

➡ teeth rather than a beak

➡ three claws on each hand

➡ a flat chest; belly ribs

➡ a long, stiff tail

Some characteristics it shared with birds:

➡ feathers

➡ a small, light body with hollow bones

➡ a wishbone

➡ short fingers

FEATHER FACT

In 2012, a group of graduate students studying an *Archaeopteryx* feather under an electron microscope isolated color cells and compared them to similar cells in modern birds. Their conclusion was that the feather they tested was dark black, though other feathers on *Archaeopteryx* may have been different colors.

DR. JOE SAYS

Birds are dinosaurs. There is no debate about this; it has been accepted for several decades by nearly all paleontologists. The definition of birds and dinosaurs does not hinge on flight; it has to do with subtle differences in the skeleton. There are birds that do not fly and there were non-bird dinosaurs that could fly.

— *Dr. Joseph Sertich, Paleontologist*

The word *sharp* describes *Troodon*'s eyesight, teeth, and intelligence. Its eyes were large and on the sides of its head, which probably gave it acute vision over a large area. Its knifelike serrated teeth could rip into prey. And its brain—big relative to its small body size—may have made it a good hunter. It hunted in packs to attack and kill much larger prey.

FOSSIL FILE

Troodon had one of the biggest ratios of body mass to brain of all dinosaurs, indicating intelligence. Scientists think that its intelligence was close to that of modern birds such as eagles and hawks.

SAFE HAVENS

A group of *Troodon* nests, found in Montana with fossilized eggs and embryos inside, showed that *Troodon* was careful and smart about how it hatched its young. The nests were built in soft earth. They were all shaped like teardrops, with protective rims around them. Scientists were able to determine that two eggs were laid at a time, and additional eggs were added every few days; the female then brooded (sat on) the entire clutch at once. It took 45–60 days for the eggs to hatch.

A pack of small Troodon *attack a large* Torosaurus.

DID YOU KNOW?

Troodon hatchlings had strong leg bones, which meant they were probably able to run right after they hatched.

PALEO DATA

TROODON

PRONUNCIATION

TROH-uh-don

SIZE

6–7 feet long; weighed 110 pounds

AGE

Late Cretaceous, about 75 million years ago

LOCATION

Western North America

FOSSILS

Many skeletons and teeth

DIET

Meat

The Lay of the Land

When dinosaurs first appeared, the land on Earth was one big continent called Pangaea, and some areas may have been too dry to support life. By the Jurassic period, the big landmass was breaking up and there were bodies of water in new places. Mountains, swamps, and coastlines became dinosaur habitats. Dinosaurs were also common on the plains where plants were plentiful, especially in later periods.

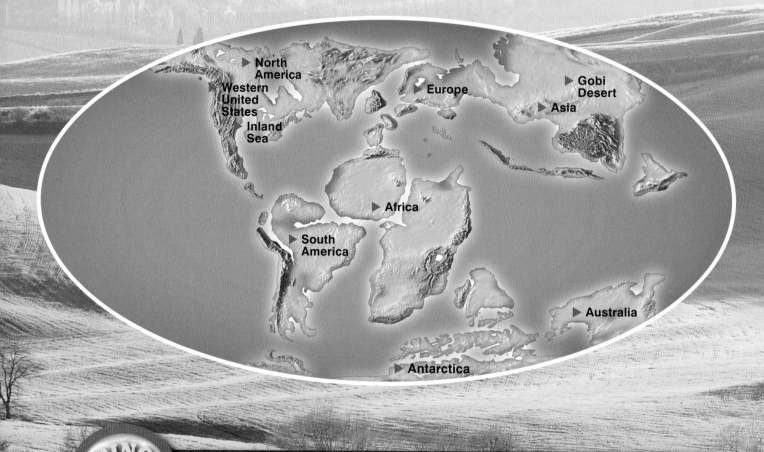

North America
Western United States
Inland Sea
Europe
Gobi Desert
Asia
Africa
South America
Australia
Antarctica

WHERE TO LOOK

Paleontologists travel all over the world looking for dinosaur bones. Often they concentrate in areas that are rich in fossils, such as the Morrison Formation in the western United States, or the Gobi desert in Mongolia. Other times, an unexpected fossil discovery—by construction workers or miners, for example—leads them to investigate a new area. Junior paleontologists—kids who love dinosaurs—can find evidence of dinosaur life in parks and preserves that have special exhibits for visitors.

Over the 186 million years that dinosaurs lived on Earth, the continents shifted and new places to live were formed. Dinosaurs gathered in habitats that fulfilled their needs for food, water, and shelter.

FORESTS

Lush forests filled with evergreen trees, ferns, and cycads (short, palmlike plants), were common in South America and the western United States. Some of the most notable fossil beds, such as the Morrison Formation, were covered in these forests. They provided food for herbivores and cover for carnivores that hunted them.

SHORELINES

A lot of dinosaurs lived along the shore during the Cretaceous period, but the shoreline was not where it is today. The southwestern United States—Colorado, Utah, New Mexico—was located on the edge of a great inland sea. Every kind of dinosaur—big meat-eaters, huge sauropods, heavy stegosaurs and ceratopsids, fast ornithopods—was found along shorelines in North America and other continents.

SWAMPS AND RIVERSIDES

In the Late Jurassic and Early Cretaceous periods, wetlands covered much of Europe and North America. Primitive plants thrived in those areas and were excellent food sources for herbivores. Carnivores flocked to swamps and riversides to eat the herbivores that lived there. Fish-eating carnivores such as *Spinosaurus* also lived in swamps.

DESERTS

Dry areas and deserts were not the easiest habitats for animals to survive, and fewer fossils have been found in areas that had these conditions during the Age of Dinosaurs. *Protoceratops* and *Velociraptor*—the famous fighting pair of fossils—were found in the Gobi desert, showing that some dinosaurs managed life in the deserts of Asia, maybe in oases between sand dunes.

Home Is Where the Food Is

Several elements were necessary to make a prehistoric habitat successful—climate, landscape, availability of water—but the most important factor was food. Herbivores needed to find habitats where plants were plentiful and easy to reach. Carnivores looked for places where there were herbivores for them to eat. The scene below depicts what may have happened when food became scarce.

ON THE SCENE

As it browses in a familiar field, *Camptosaurus* searches and searches for small shrubs and ferns to eat. There aren't as many as yesterday, and the field was full when the sun was higher in the sky.

Camptosaurus and its family have all become thinner. They need more time each day to find the hundreds of pounds of plants they need to survive. It is hot; the sun blazes over them, making them thirsty for water, but the streams have dried up. It is time to move to another place, to higher, cooler ground. The trek begins; hundreds of *Camptosaurus* join a herd and head north.

WORD

Migration is a journey by animals from one region to another, often in search of more food or water. A migration can be seasonal or permanent.

PLANTS IN DINOSAUR HABITATS

EVERGREEN TREES The leaves and bark of slow-growing evergreens such as yews, pines, redwoods, and monkey-puzzle trees provided year-round nourishment. Evergreens were a prime food source for sauropods.

CYCADS In the Late Triassic and Early Jurassic periods, low-growing cycads (plants that looked like short palm trees), were available to dinosaurs in warmer areas. They had tough leaves and soft bark that early prosauropods devoured.

FERNS AND OTHER LEAFY PLANTS
Horsetails and ferns grew quickly and were always available. In addition to the leaves themselves, the seeds and spores were food for dinosaurs.

FLOWERING PLANTS Flowering plants appeared in the Cretaceous period; by the Late Cretaceous, many new dinosaurs had appeared to eat them. Among prehistoric flowering plants were bayberry, laurel, and magnolia.

THE IMPORTANCE OF PLANTS

Plants were not only a food source; they also improved the atmosphere. Plants gave off oxygen when they converted carbon dioxide to make food. As Earth became more dense with plants, long before dinosaurs, the oxygen levels rose and it was easier for animals to become more highly evolved.

Sauropods were gigantic lizard-hipped, plant-eating dinosaurs with consistent body shapes: enormous torsos on four thick limbs. They had clawed, lizardlike feet. Their big size helped them ward off predators and gave them extra storage capacity for food so that they could extract more nutrients from plants through fermentation. The fossil record shows that there were about ten times as many sauropods as meat-eating theropods that hunted them, so enough sauropods were able to live and create future generations of dinosaur babies successfully.

▶ All four limbs were big and sturdy, and the front limbs were used as feet. Each foot had claws, but they weren't very sharp.

TIMELINE

LATE TRIASSIC

227 TO 201
MILLION YEARS AGO

Primitive sauropods, including *Eoraptor*, appeared; some still ate meat and walked on two legs.

EARLY JURASSIC

201 TO 180
MILLION YEARS AGO

The first "true" sauropods—eusauropods—developed the typical sauropod body. *Barapasaurus*, a eusauropod, lived in what is now India.

MIDDLE JURASSIC

180 TO 159
MILLION YEARS AGO

Sauropods started to achieve their legendary size. *Abrosaurus*, a big nose dinosaur with large nostrils, lived during this period.

Sauropods

▶ Sauropods had very long necks and tails supported by many vertebrae.

Diplodocus skeleton showing size compared to humans

AT A GLANCE

The name *sauropod* comes from a Greek word meaning "lizard feet." Sauropod fossils have been found on all seven continents. There are 198 known sauropods.

Sauropods were:
➡ part of the saurischian (lizard-hipped) order of dinosaurs
➡ quadrupedal
➡ herbivores

Sauropods are divided into four sections in this book:

Early Sauropods
➡ Some were omnivores that ate meat and plants, such as *Massospondylus*
➡ Some walked on two feet

Giant Sauropods
➡ Had large nostrils on the tops of their heads
➡ Some grew to 85 feet long

Titanic Lizards
➡ Survived to the end of the Age of Dinosaurs
➡ Included the largest dinosaur ever, *Argentinosaurus*

Whiptail Lizards
➡ Included some of the longest dinosaurs, such as *Diplodocus* and *Apatosaurus*
➡ Had tails that could be used like whips

Some well-known sauropods: *Brachiosaurus, Apatosaurus*

LATE JURASSIC

159 TO 144
MILLION YEARS AGO

Herds of huge sauropods roamed the Earth. One of them was *Brachiosaurus*, which grew to 85 feet.

EARLY CRETACEOUS

144 TO 98
MILLION YEARS AGO

Huge sauropods continued to thrive. Though some, like *Brachiosaurus* and *Diplodocus*, died out, a new group of giants called titanosaurs appeared.

LATE CRETACEOUS

98 TO 66
MILLION YEARS AGO

The largest sauropods, including *Argentinosaurus*, appeared. All the sauropods, along with all other dinosaurs, became extinct.

PROSAUROPODS

	SIZE	AGE	FOSSILS	LOCATION
Aardonyx (*AR*-doh-niks)	M	EJ	Partial skeleton	AF
Adeopapposaurus (ad-ee-oh-*PAP*-oh-sore-us)	UN	EJ	Partial skeleton	SA
Ammosaurus (*AM*-oh-sore-us)	M	EJ	Partial skeleton	NA
Anchisaurus (*AN*-key-sore-us)	S	EJ	Partial skeleton	NA
Chromogisaurus (kroh-moh-gee-*SORE*-us)	XS	LT	Partial skeleton	SA
Coloradisaurus (coll-uh-rahd-ih-*SORE*-us)	M	LT	Skull, Bone	SA
Efraasia (eff-*RAY*-zha)	M	LT	Bone	EU
Eoraptor (*EE*-oh-rap-tore)	XS	LT	Skull, Bone	SA
Eucnemesaurus (yook-*NEE*-mee-sore-us)	XL	LT	Partial skeleton	AF
Glacialisaurus (*GLAY*-see-al-ih-sore-us)	L	EJ	Bone	AN
Guaibasaurus (*GWAI*-bah-sore-us)	S	LT	Partial skeleton	SA
Ignavusaurus (ig-*NAY*-voo-sore-us)	S	EJ	Partial skeleton	AF
Jingshanosaurus (jing-sha-noh-*SORE*-us)	L	EJ	Partial skeleton	AS
Leonerasaurus (*LEE*-oh-neh-rah-sore-us)	UN	MJ	Teeth, Bone	SA
Leyesaurus (lay-uh-*SORE*-us)	S	EJ	Skull, Bone	SA
Lufengosaurus (loo-*FUHN*-go-sore-us)	M	EJ	Full skeleton	AS
Massospondylus (mas-oh-*SPON*-dih-lus)	M	EJ	Full skeleton	AS
Mussaurus (moo-*SORE*-us)	S	LT	Skull, Bone	SA
Nambalia (nam-*BAL*-ee-uh)	UN	LT	Skull	AS
Panphagia (pan-*FAY*-gee-uh)	XS	LT	Skull, Bone	SA
Pantydraco (pant-uh-*DRAY*-co)	S	EJ	Partial skeleton	EU
Plateosauravus (*PLAY*-tee-oh-sore-uh-vuss)	UN	LT	Partial skeleton	AF
Plateosaurus (*PLAY*-tee-oh-*SORE*-us)	L	LT	Full skeleton	EU
Riojasaurus (*REE*-oh-hah-sore-us)	XL	LT	Partial skeleton	SA
Ruehleia (*ROO*-eh-lee-a)	L	LT	Partial skeleton	EU
Sarahsaurus (sa-ruh-*SORE*-us)	M	EJ	Partial skeleton	NA
Saturnalia (sa-tur-*NAY*-lee-uh)	S	LT	Teeth, Partial skeleton	SA
Seitaad (say-*EE*-tad)	M	MJ	Partial skeleton	NA
Thecodontosaurus (*THEEH*-co-dahn-toe-sore-us)	S	LT	Partial skeleton	EU
Unaysaurus (oo-*NAH*-ee-sore-us)	S	LT	Partial skeleton	SA
Yunnanosaurus (yoo-*NA*-noh-sore-us)	L	EJ	Full skeleton	AS

BASAL SAUROPOD

	SIZE	AGE	FOSSILS	LOCATION
Antetonitrus (an-tee-*TON*-ee-trus)	XL	LT	Bone	AF
Blikanasaurus (blih-*KAH*-nuh-sore-us)	M	LT	Bone	AF

	SIZE	AGE	FOSSILS	LOCATION
Camelotia (kam-eh-*LOH*-tee-ah)	L	LT	Partial skeleton	EU
Gongxianosaurus (*GONG*-she-yen-o-sore-us)	XXL	EJ	Partial skeleton	AS
Isanosaurus (ee-*SAHN*-no-sore-us)	L	LT	Partial skeleton	AS
Lessemsaurus (*LES*-um-sore-us)	XL	LT	Bone	SA
Melanorosaurus (*MEH*-la-nor-oh-sore-us)	XL	LT	Skull, Bone	AF
Tazoudasaurus (*TAH*-zou-duh-sore-us)	L	MJ	Partial skeleton	AF
Vulcanodon (vull-*KAN*-uh-don)	M	EJ	Partial skeleton	AF

BASAL EUSAUROPODS

	SIZE	AGE	FOSSILS	LOCATION
Abrosaurus (ab-roh-*SORE*-us)	L	MJ	Partial skeleton	AS
Algoasaurus (al-*GO*-uh-sore-us)	L	LJ/EC	Bone	AF
Amygdalodon (a-mig-*DAH*-loh-don)	M	MJ	Teeth	SA
Asiatosaurus (*AY*-zhah-toe-sore-us)	UN	EC	Teeth	AS
Atlasaurus (*AT*-luh-sore-us)	XXL	MJ	Partial skeleton	AF
Barapasaurus (buh-*RA*-pah-sore-us)	XXL	EJ	Partial skeleton	AS
Cetiosaurus (see-*TIE*-o-sore-us)	XXL	MJ	Partial skeleton	EU/AF
Chebsaurus (cheb-*SORE*-us)	L	MJ	Partial skeleton	AF
Chuanjiesaurus (*CHU*-wahn-gee-sore-us)	XXL	MJ	Bone	AS
Eomamenchisaurus (ee-oh-*MAH*-men-chee-sore-us)	XL	MJ	Partial skeleton	AS
Ferganasaurus (fur-*GAH*-na-sore-us)	XXL	LJ	Bone	AS
Hudiesaurus (*HOO*-dee-eh-sore-us)	XXL	LJ	Partial skeleton	AS
Jobaria (joh-*BAHR*-ee-uh)	XXL	EC	Full skeleton	AF
Mamenchisaurus (mah-*MEN*-chee-sore-us)	XXL	LJ	Partial skeleton	AS
Nebulasaurus (neh-byoo-luh-*SORE*-us)	UN	MJ	Skull	AS
Omeisaurus (*OH*-may-sore-us)	XXL	LJ	Partial skeleton	AS
Patagosaurus (*PAT*-uh-go-sore-us)	XXL	MJ	Partial skeleton	SA
Pukyongosaurus (*POO*-kyong-oh-sore-us)	XXL	EC	Bone	AS
Qinlingosaurus (chin-ling-oh-*SORE*-us)	XXL	LC	Bone	AS
Rhoetosaurus (*REE*-toe-sore-us)	XL	MJ	Bone	AU
Shunosaurus (*SHOO*-no-sore-us)	XL	MJ	Full skeleton	AS
Tienshanosaurus (tee-en-*SHAN*-oh-sore-us)	XL	LJ	Partial skeleton	AS
Xianshanosaurus (zan-shan-oh-*SORE*-us)	UN	LC	Bone	AS
Xinjiangtitan (*SHEE*-jee-yong-tie-tuhn)	XXL	MJ	Partial skeleton	AS
Yuanmousaurus (yoo-ahn-moo-*SORE*-us)	XXL	MJ	Partial skeleton	AS
Zby (*zee-bee*)	XXL	LJ	Partial skeleton	EU

LEGEND

Featured dinosaurs are set in red in the list above.

SIZE
XS	Under 5 feet
S	5-10 feet
M	10-20 feet
L	20-30 feet
XL	30-40 feet
XXL	Over 40 feet
UN	Unknown

AGE (years ago)
LT	Late Triassic (227-201 million)
EJ	Early Jurassic (201-180 million)
MJ	Middle Jurassic (180-159 million)
LJ	Late Jurassic (159-144 million)
EC	Early Cretaceous (144-98 million)
LC	Late Cretaceous (98-66 million)

FOSSILS
- Full skeleton
- Partial skeleton
- Skull
- Bone
- Teeth

LOCATION
AS	Asia
AF	Africa
EU	Europe
AU	Australia
NA	North America
SA	South America
AN	Antarctica

Early Sauropods

Barapasaurus

Sauropods didn't burst onto the prehistoric scene with all their characteristics in place. Some of the earliest ones, including *Massospondylus*, ate meat and walked on two legs—not traits we associate with sauropods. The earliest ones, such as *Vulcanodon*, were large compared to other animals of the time, but smaller than the giants that followed. Over millions of years, primitive basal sauropods evolved into gigantic dinosaurs—the largest animals that ever walked on land.

The earliest sauropods included omnivores and herbivores, and some were bipedal. Over millions of years, they grew bigger and began walking on all fours. Their digestive systems evolved and their diet shifted to eating only plants.

EORAPTOR

➡ A bipedal carnivore that was small and lightweight

➡ Name means "dawn thief" (Eos was the Greek goddess of the dawn), because it appeared at the dawn of the Age of Dinosaurs

➡ Was 5–10 feet long; weighed 20 pounds

➡ Had five fingers on each hand, three toes on each foot, and a long tail

FUN FACT *Eoraptor* was one of the earliest dinosaurs, and was a rare non-theropod that ate meat.

DR. JOE SAYS

When *Eoraptor* was first discovered, it was thought to be one of the earliest theropod dinosaurs because of its meat-eating teeth and strong hind legs. After more discoveries of *Eoraptor* and other very early sauropods, we now think that *Eoraptor* is one of the earliest sauropods. Theropods and sauropods are very closely related to each other, and their common ancestor probably looked very similar to *Eoraptor*. There are just enough sauropod features in *Eoraptor* to push it to the sauropod side of the family tree.
— *Dr. Joseph Sertich, Paleontologist*

DINO DETECTIVE

LOOKING FOR FOSSILS

In the field, paleontologists use their eyes to scan a large area, and then look more closely at a smaller area. Examining any disturbance in the rocks—a part that is a different color or sticking out—might reveal a fossil. Though they know what to look for, paleontologists say that patience and luck are more important than skill in finding fossils.

MASSOSPONDYLUS

➡ A bipedal omnivore that could also walk on all fours

➡ Named for the massive vertebrae that were the first fossils found (*masso* means "large" and *spondylos* means "vertebrae" in Greek)

➡ Was 13–20 feet long; weighed about 300 pounds

➡ Teeth indicated a diet of mostly plants but also some meat, fish, and insects

FUN FACT A *Massospondylus* nesting site with at least ten nests was discovered in 2012 in South Africa, and included nearly three dozen fossilized eggs in each nest, as well as hatchling footprints.

VULCANODON

➡ A quadrupedal herbivore that was on the small side for a sauropod

➡ Named for the lava flow where it was discovered (Vulcanus was the Roman god of fire) and for teeth found nearby but later discovered to belong to a different dinosaur (*odon* means "tooth" in Greek)

➡ Was about 20 feet long; may have weighed up to 8,000 pounds (too few fossils have been found to be certain)

➡ Had a stout body and four big legs like an elephant's

FUN FACT Only one discovery of *Vulcanodon* fossils has been made so far, in Zimbabwe in eastern Africa.

Herds and Packs

When large numbers of dinosaur skeletons are found together, it indicates that those dinosaurs may have lived in a group. Living in groups had many benefits: It allowed dinosaurs to better protect their young, to hunt more effectively, and to guard themselves against predators.

A DINOSAUR'S SOCIAL LIFE

There is a lot of social activity in the animal herds that live in the world today, and paleontologists infer that the same was true for dinosaurs. Dinosaurs found possible mates, competed for them with rivals, and courted them with rituals. Dinosaur nests have been found grouped together, so giving birth was part of herd life in some species. Protecting young, sick, and old members from attack was another herd activity. And if dinosaur herds were like modern herds, there were leaders, followers, and battles for position.

NEWS FLASH

Scientists had always thought *Triceratops* was a loner; whenever its bones were found, each site had only one skeleton. But in 2013, four 20-foot-long *Triceratops* skeletons were found in Wyoming, showing that at least some of these herbivores died while in a group.

Some dinosaurs were loners, but some interacted with one another to find food and for protection. Interaction was always necessary to create offspring.

PACKS

Unlike herds, which protected their members and improved the chances of survival for all, packs were made up of predators that joined together to hunt more efficiently. Fossil discoveries show pack behavior. The carnivores were not big enough to win battles with the larger herbivores on their own, but together they could bring prey down.

HOW DID DINOSAURS SLEEP?

While no one knows for sure how dinosaurs slept, sleeping in groups would have provided protection. Experts think dinosaurs probably slept in short bursts. Carnivores would have needed to rest after hunting; scientists think that they slept lying down. Huge sauropods probably slept standing up, like elephants do—getting up and down is hard for an animal with a massive body.

Courtship and Mating

In order for a species to survive, every generation has to create the next generation. Animals, including humans, find appropriate mates so that babies can be born.

MATING RITUALS

Many animals, especially birds, have developed elaborate rituals to let the opposite sex know that they are interested in mating. Some animals raise and lower their heads; some shake their tail feathers; some dance around in circles. Dinosaurs had body parts that would have been useful in these rituals.

Cryolophosaurus's head crest may have been used to attract mates.

Citipati *in a feather-shaking mating ritual*

Two Gigantoraptor *in a mating dance*

SAILS *Spinosaurus's* flashy fan-shaped sail may have attracted mates.

NECKS AND TAILS *Supersaurus's* long neck and whiplike tail may have been used in mating rituals.

BONE UP!

How do we know if a dinosaur was male or female? Experts made an exciting discovery in 2005.

They found that a dinosaur skeleton had a type of reduced-calcium bone material that female birds also have. If a female dinosaur was creating eggs, it borrowed calcium from its bones to build the shell. Now experts know that any skeleton with reduced calcium in its bones was a female. But the absence of that type of bone isn't proof that a dinosaur was male, since females only used extra calcium when they were breeding.

DETAILS
32 GIANT SAUROPODS

MACRONARIA

	SIZE	AGE	FOSSILS	LOCATION
Abrosaurus (*A-broh*-sore-*us*)	L	MJ		AS
Aragosaurus (*a-rah-go-**SORE**-us*)	XXL	EC		EU
Camarasaurus (***KAM**-a-rah-sore-us*)	XXL	LJ		NA
Dongbeititan (***DONG**-beh-tie-tan*)	XXL	EC		AS
Janenschia (*yah-**NEN**-chee-ah*)	XXL	LJ		AF
Lusotitan (*loo-soh-**TIE**-tan*)	XXL	LJ		EU
Tehuelchesaurus (*tay-**WAYL**-chay-sore-us*)	XXL	LJ		SA

EARLY TITANS: BRACHIOSAURS

	SIZE	AGE	FOSSILS	LOCATION
Abydosaurus (*ah-**BEE**-doh-sore-us*)	XXL	LJ		NA
Australodocus (*aw-stra-**LOH**-do-cus*)	XXL	LJ		AF
Baotianmansaurus (*bow-shan-man-**SORE**-us*)	XXL	LC		AS
Brachiosaurus (***BRA**-key-oh-sore-us*)	XXL	LJ		NA
Cedarosaurus (*see-dur-oh-**SORE**-us*)	XXL	EC		NA
Daanosaurus (***DA**-no-sore-us*)	M	LJ		AS
Duriatitan (***DOO**-ree-uh-tie-tan*)	XXL	LJ		EU
Europasaurus (*yoo-**RO**-puh-sore-us*)	M	LJ		EU
Fukuititan (*foo-**KOO**-ee-tie-tan*)	XXL	EC		AS
Fusuisaurus (***FOO**-soo-ee-sore-us*)	XXL	EC		AS
Giraffatitan (*jih-**RAF**-uh-tie-tan*)	XXL	LJ		AF
Jiutaisaurus (*joo-**TAH**-ee-**SORE**-us*)	L	MC		AS
Ornithopsis (*or-nih-**THOP**-sis*)	M	EC		EU
Sonorasaurus (*sun-**OR**-uh-sore-us*)	XXL	MC		NA
Venenosaurus (*ve-**NEE**-no-sore-us*)	L	EC		NA

EARLY TITANS, SOMPHOSPONDYLI

	SIZE	AGE	FOSSILS	LOCATION
Agustinia (*ah-**GOO**-stee-nee-a*)	XXL	EC		SA
Angolatitan (*an-go-la-**TIE**-tan*)	XXL	LC		AF
Astrophocaudia (*a-stroh-foe-**CAW**-dee-uh*)	XXL	EC		NA
Brontomerus (*bron-toe-**MARE**-us*)	L	EC		NA
Diamantinasaurus (*die-uh-man-tin-uh-**SORE**-us*)	XXL	EC		AU
Huanghetitan (*hwah-en-gie-**TIE**-tan*)	XXL	EC		AS
Ligabuesaurus (*li-gay-**BWAY**-sore-us*)	XXL	EC		SA
Liubangosaurus (*loo-bang-oh-**SORE**-us*)	XXL	EC		AS
Malarguesaurus (***MA**-lar-gway-sore-us*)	XXL	LC		SA
Pelorosaurus (*peh-**LOH**-roh-sore-us*)	XXL	EC		EU

Abrosaurus

LEGEND
Featured dinosaurs are set in red in the list above.

SIZE
- XS Under 5 feet
- S 5-10 feet
- M 10-20 feet
- L 20-30 feet
- XL 30-40 feet
- XXL Over 40 feet
- UN Unknown

AGE (years ago)
- LT Late Triassic (227-201 million)
- EJ Early Jurassic (201-180 million)
- MJ Middle Jurassic (180-159 million)
- LJ Late Jurassic (159-144 million)
- EC Early Cretaceous (144-98 million)
- LC Late Cretaceous (98-66 million)

FOSSILS
- Full skeleton
- Partial skeleton
- Skull
- Bone
- Teeth

LOCATION
- AS Asia
- AF Africa
- EU Europe
- AU Australia
- NA North America
- SA South America
- AN Antarctica

Giant Sauropods
Big Noses

This group is also called macronaria (*macro* means "big," *naria* means "nostrils"). A recognizable feature of this group was big nostrils on the top of the head. These sauropods of the Middle Jurassic period, including *Brachiosaurus* and *Camarasaurus*, had developed the classic sauropod body—a superlong neck and tail with a small head. And they were beginning to achieve the legendary size of the sauropods that followed them millions of years later.

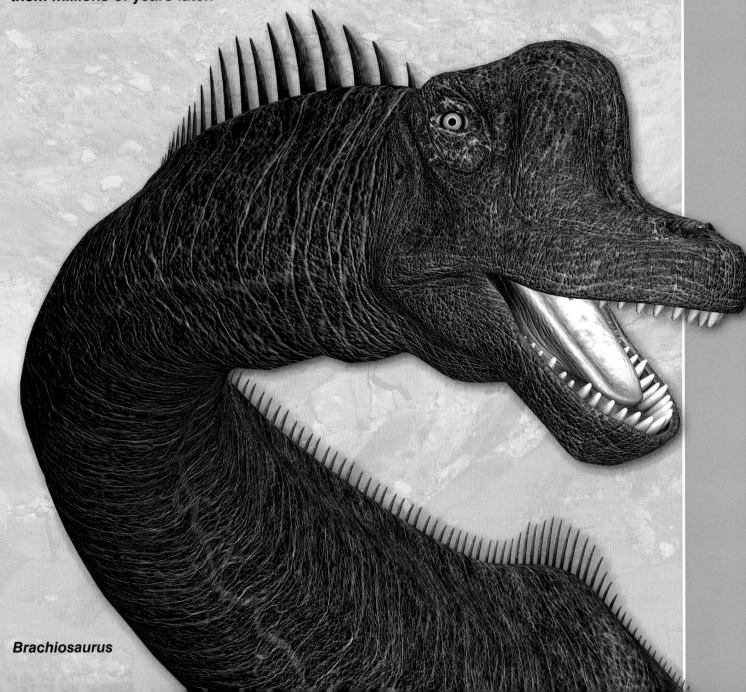

Brachiosaurus

Most sauropods had similar forms. They had small heads on superlong necks, big bellies to hold all the plants they ate, long forearms that served as front legs, and very long tails. Many look very similar to each other and often confuse paleontologists.

GIRAFFATITAN

➡ A quadrupedal herbivore with a long, graceful neck

➡ Name means "giant giraffe" (*titano* means "giant" in Greek)

➡ Was 80 feet long; weighed about 60,000–75,000 pounds

➡ Its neck, fully extended, would reach 40 feet off the ground, about the height of a four-story building

FUN FACT *Giraffatitan* was initially thought to be a *Brachiosaurus*, but further study showed that it had enough differences to be given its own name in 2009.

FOSSIL FILE

The tallest mounted dinosaur skeleton in the world is a *Giraffatitan* in the Museum für Naturkunde in Berlin. The skeleton, which has been certified by the Guinness Book of World Records, is a re-creation made from fossils of several different specimens.

SONORASAURUS

➡ A quadrupedal herbivore that ate tough plants with the help of gastroliths

➡ Named for the Sonoran Desert in Arizona, where the first fossils were found by University of Arizona student Richard Thompson

➡ Was about 50 feet long; weighed up to 70,000 pounds

➡ Had a long neck and was small for a sauropod

FUN FACT The first *Sonorasaurus* fossils were found in an area of the Sonoran Desert called the Chihuahuan Desert, but scientists thought *Chihuahuasaurus* might be a poor name for a 50-foot giant.

CAMARASAURUS

➡ A quadrupedal herbivore that ate tough, fibrous plants

➡ Name means "chambered lizard" in Greek

➡ Was 50–75 feet long; weighed up to 95,000 pounds

➡ Had chambered, or hollowed-out, vertebrae, and a short neck and tail

FUN FACT Fossilized tracks show that *Camarasaurus* traveled in herds and covered long distances, probably moving to other regions when food or water became scarce.

PALEO DATA

BRACHIOSAURUS

PRONUNCIATION
BRA-key-oh-sore-us

SIZE
80–85 feet long; weighed about 100,000 pounds

AGE
Late Jurassic, about 150 million years ago

LOCATION
Western North America

FOSSILS
Several partial skeletons

DIET
Plants

Brachiosaurus's arms were longer than its legs by more than a foot. Since the dinosaur walked on all four limbs, its long arms (*brachia* means "arms") gave it a distinct posture similar to a giraffe's, with its shoulders and neck higher than its back. *Brachiosaurus* fossils were found in an area known as the Morrison Formation in western North America. In this semidesert region, tall trees grew along narrow rivers. This huge dinosaur would have been able to reach the tops of the trees without even stretching its long neck.

FUN FACT

An asteroid was named after *Brachiosaurus* in 1991. It orbits the sun once every four and a half years.

LONG NECK

Brachiosaurus had a very long neck—up to 40 feet. In order to keep its neck fully extended all the time, it would have needed a very strong heart. To get blood all the way up to its head, it may have needed complex valves and pumps in its neck arteries. Long, sturdy legs helped support the weight of its neck.

? DID YOU KNOW?

For many years, scientists thought that *Brachiosaurus* and its family lived in water. A watery living environment would have made it easier to move the huge body, and the large nostrils, high on the head, would have poked out of the water. The theory was that *Brachiosaurus* waded in water up to 40 feet deep and used its head like a snorkel for breathing. Later studies showed that the water pressure at that depth would have killed it, so this big herbivore is now known to have been a land animal.

Getting Around

Dinosaurs had many ways of getting from place to place. They walked and ran on two legs or four; some could run very fast and some lumbered along at a pace that was slower than human walking. Scientists believe that most dinosaurs could swim when necessary, and some dinosaurs could fly.

FOOTPRINT FOSSILS

Dinosaur footprints were preserved when the soft earth in which they were made became fossilized. Paleontologists can guess which dinosaur made which tracks by comparing them with fossils of the feet of known dinosaurs from the same time period. Sometimes, thousands of footprints have been found in an area; that tells scientists that the dinosaurs that left the tracks traveled in herds or packs. A large group of footprints leading in the same direction is called a trackway. Some trackways continue for many miles, indicating a group of dinosaurs took a long journey.

EVERYONE IN THE WATER!

Living animals that have bodies similar to dinosaurs—such as horses or hippopotamuses—usually can swim. So paleontologists think that dinosaurs could swim when they had to. In the past few years, dinosaur tracks found in now-dry rivers in Spain, Wyoming, and China have proved that dinosaurs did indeed spend time in shallow water. The evidence shows that these tracks became shallower as the water became deeper, because the water made the dinosaur's body lighter.

Scientists can learn a lot from the size, depth, and distance between dinosaur tracks. By measuring the depth of the footprint, they can tell how much a dinosaur weighed, if the dinosaur walked on two or four legs, and how fast the dinosaur walked or ran.

UNEARTHING

Dinosaur fossils are very fragile. Though these bones have survived for millions of years underground, they can disintegrate when exposed to air. Paleontologists take great care when lifting fossils from the ground. To gently remove newly discovered bones, the soil is brushed off and around a fossil, and then the surrounding dirt is dug out until the bone can be lifted carefully out of the ground.

DINO DETECTIVE

Locomotion—or moving from place to place—was essential for dinosaurs to find food and escape predators. They developed good methods for getting around.

HOW FAST COULD DINOSAURS RUN?

SAUROPODS
About 3 miles per hour

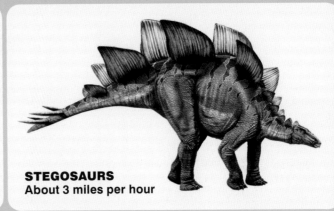

STEGOSAURS
About 3 miles per hour

TYRANNOSAURUS REX AND OTHER LARGE THEROPODS
Up to 15 miles per hour

IGUANADON AND OTHER ORNITHOPODS
Up to 25 miles per hour

VELOCIRAPTOR AND OTHER BIRDLIKE THEROPODS
Up to 40 miles per hour

DETAILS
71 TITANIC LIZARDS SAUROPODS

TITANOSAURS

Name	Size	Age	Fossils	Location
Amargatitanis (a-mar-gah-tie-**TAN**-iss)	XL	EC	Bone	SA
Ampelosaurus (**AM**-puhl-oh-sore-us)	XXL	LC	Bone	EU
Andesaurus (an-dee-**SORE**-us)	XXL	LC	Bone	SA
Argyrosaurus (**AR**-gear-oh-sore-us)	XXL	LC	Bone	SA
Atacamatitan (**A**-tuh-cuh-muh-tie-tan)	XXL	LC	Bone	SA
Atsinganosaurus (at-sing-a-no-**SORE**-us)	XXL	LC	Bone	EU
Austrosaurus (**AW**-stroh-sore-us)	XXL	EC	Teeth/Skull	AU
Balochisaurus (bah-lo-chee-**SORE**-us)	XXL	LC	Bone	SA
Barrosasaurus (**BAR**-oh-suh-sore-us)	XXL	LC	Bone	SA
Baurutitan (**BAH**-roo-tie-tan)	XXL	LC	Bone	SA
Brohisaurus (**BRO**-he-sore-us)	XXL	LJ	Bone	AS
Campylodoniscus (**CAM**-pee-loh-doh-niss-kus)	XXL	LC	Teeth, Bone	SA
Chubutisaurus (shoo-**BOO**-tee-sore-us)	XXL	EC	Partial skeleton	SA
Drusilasaura (**DROO**-sill-uh-sore-uh)	L	LC	Bone	SA
Futalongkosaurus (**FOO**-tah-long-koh-sore-us)	XXL	LC	Partial skeleton	SA
Gobititan (**GO**-bee-tie-tan)	XL	EC	Bone	AS
Hypselosaurus (**HIP**-seh-loh-sore-us)	L	LC	Bone	EU
Iuticosaurus (**YOO**-tih-koh-sore-us)	XXL	EC	Bone	EU
Jiangshanosaurus (**JEE**-ahng-shan-oh-sore-us)	XXL	LC	Bone	AS
Karongasaurus (**CAR**-ohn-guh-sore-us)	L	EC	Teeth, Bone	AF
Khetranisaurus (**KEH**-tra-nee-sore-us)	XXL	LC	Bone	AS
Laplatasaurus (lah-**PLAH**-tah-sore-us)	XXL	LC	Bone	SA/AF
Macrurosaurus (ma-**KROO**-roh-sore-us)	XL	EC	Partial skeleton	EU
Magyarosaurus (**MA**-ghee-yah-roh-sore-us)	M	LC	Bone	EU
Marisaurus (mair-ee-**SORE**-us)	XXL	LC	Skull, Bone	AS
Mendozasaurus (men-**DOZE**-uh-sore-us)	XXL	EC	Bone	SA
Microcoelus (my-**CRO**-see-luss)	L	EC	Bone	SA
Pakisaurus (pa-kee-**SORE**-us)	XXL	LC	Bone	AS
Paludititan (pah-**LOO**-dih-tie-tan)	M	LC	Partial skeleton	EU
Paralatitan (pah-ral-uh-**TIE**-tan)	XXL	EC	Bone	AF
Puertasaurus (pwear-ta-**SORE**-us)	XXL	LC	Bone	SA
Qingxiusaurus (**CHING**-shoo-sore-us)	XXL	LC	Bone	AS
Quetecsaurus (**KEW**-tek-sore-us)	UN	LC	Partial skeleton	SA
Ruyangosaurus (**ROO**-yang-oh-sore-us)	XXL	LC	Bone	AS
Sauroposeidon (**SORE**-oh-po-sy-don)	XXL	EC	Bone	NA
Sulaimanisaurus (**SOO**-lay-man-ee-sore-us)	XXL	LC	Bone	AS
Tangvayosaurus (tahng-**VY**-oh-sore-us)	XXL	EC	Partial skeleton	AS
Titanosaurus (tie-**TAN**-oh-sore-us)	L	LC	Bone	AS
Traukutitan (**TROH**-koo-tie-tan)	XL	LC	Bone	SA
Uberabatitan (oo-**BA**-ruh-ba-tie-tan)	L	LC	Partial skeleton	SA
Vahiny (**VAH**-heen)	UN	LC	Bone	AF
Wintonotitan (**WIN**-ton-oh-tie-tan)	XXL	LC	Bone	AU
Yongjinglong (young-jeeng-long)	L	EC	Bone	AS

LITHOSTROTIANS

Name	Size	Age	Fossils	Location
Admantisaurus (ad-man-tih-**SORE**-us)	XXL	LC	Bone	SA
Aeolosaurus (**EE**-oh-loh-sore-us)	XXL	LC	Partial skeleton	SA
Alamosaurus (a-luh-moh-**SORE**-us)	XXL	LC	Partial skeleton	NA
Antarctosaurus (an-tark-toe-**SORE**-us)	XXL	LC	Skull, Partial skeleton	SA
Argentinosaurus (ahr-jen-**TEE**-noh-sore-us)	XXL	LC	Bone	SA
Bonatitan (**BO**-nah-tie-tan)	XL	LC	Skull, Partial skeleton	SA
Dongyangosaurus (**DONG**-yang-oh-sore-us)	XXL	LC	Partial skeleton	AS
Elaltitan (el-al-**TIE**-tan)	XXL	LC	Partial skeleton	SA
Gondwanatitan (gon-**DWAH**-nuh-tie-tan)	L	LC	Partial skeleton	SA
Huabeisaurus (hwah-bay-**SORE**-us)	XXL	LC	Teeth, Bone	AS
Isisaurus (eye-**SISS**-sore-us)	XXL	LC	Skull	AS
Janenschia (yah-**NEN**-chee-ah)	XXL	LJ	Bone	AF
Lirainosaurus (lee-**RAY**-noh-sore-us)	XXL	LC	Partial skeleton	EU
Loricosaurus (**LOH**-rih-koh-sore-us)	UN	LC	Bone	SA
Maxakalisaurus (**MAX**-uh-**KAL**-ee-sore-us)	XXL	LC	Partial skeleton	SA
Muyelensaurus (moo-yay-len-**SORE**-us)	L	LC	Skull, Bone	SA
Narambuenatitan (nuh-ram-byoo-nuh-**TIE**-tan)	XXL	LC	Partial skeleton	SA
Nemegtosaurus (**NAY**-meg-toe-sore-us)	XXL	LC	Skull	AS
Neuquensaurus (**NOO**-kwen-sore-us)	XXL	LC	Bone	SA
Overosaurus (**OH**-vuh-ro-sore-us)	L	LC	Bone	SA
Panamericansaurus (pan-uh-mair-uh-kan-**SORE**-us)	M	LC	Bone	SA
Pitekunsaurus (**PIH**-teh-kun-sore-us)	XXL	LC	Skull, Bone	SA
Quaesitosaurus (kwee-**SEE**-toh-sore-us)	XXL	LC	Skull	AS
Rapetosaurus (ruh-**PAY**-toh-sore-us)	XXL	LC	Partial skeleton	AF
Rinconsaurus (**RIN**-con-sore-us)	XXL	LC	Partial skeleton	SA
Rocasaurus (**ROH**-kah-sore-us)	L	LC	Partial skeleton	SA
Saltasaurus (**SAL**-tuh-sore-us)	XL	LC	Partial skeleton	SA
Tapuiasaurus (**TA**-pwee-uh-sore-us)	XL	EC	Partial skeleton	SA

LEGEND

Featured dinosaurs are set in red in the list above.

SIZE
- XS — Under 5 feet
- S — 5-10 feet
- M — 10-20 feet
- L — 20-30 feet
- XL — 30-40 feet
- XXL — Over 40 feet
- UN — Unknown

AGE (years ago)
- LT — Late Triassic (227-201 million)
- EJ — Early Jurassic (201-180 million)
- MJ — Middle Jurassic (180-159 million)
- LJ — Late Jurassic (159-144 million)
- EC — Early Cretaceous (144-98 million)
- LC — Late Cretaceous (98-66 million)

FOSSILS
- Full skeleton
- Partial skeleton
- Skull
- Bone
- Teeth

LOCATION
- AS — Asia
- AF — Africa
- EU — Europe
- AU — Australia
- NA — North America
- SA — South America
- AN — Antarctica

Titanic Lizards
Sauropods
The Titans

Titanosaurs, or titanic lizards (*titanic* means "giant"), appeared in the Cretaceous period and lived until dinosaurs disappeared 66 million years ago. There were dozens of different types in this group, possibly more than 100 in total. They completed the sauropod evolution to larger and larger sizes. There were a few dwarf varieties of titanic lizards, such as *Magyarosaurus*, but the largest dinosaur discovered so far—*Argentinosaurus*—is in this group.

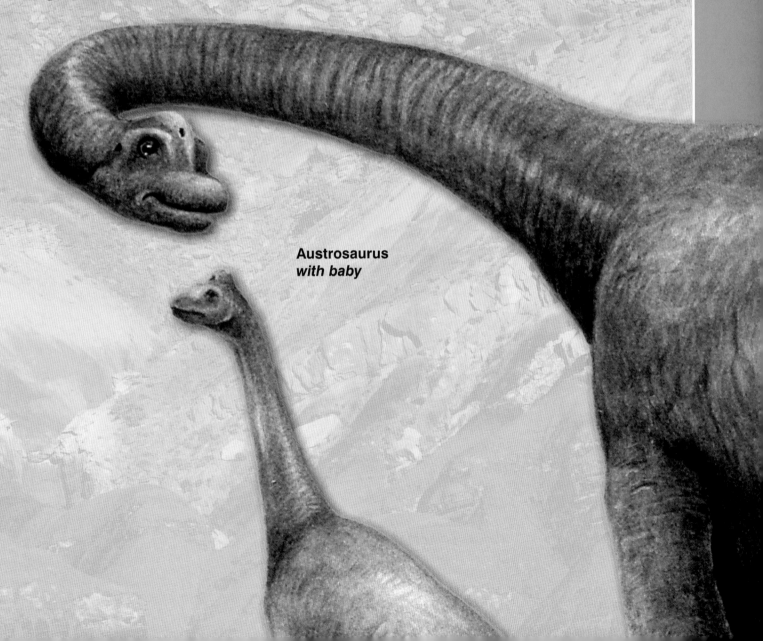

Austrosaurus
with baby

This group includes some of the largest dinosaurs ever discovered—*Argentinosaurus* is number one on the list of longest dinosaurs. Although most of the dinosaurs in this group were similar in shape, some had interesting features such as bony plates on their backs.

Crocodile osteoderms

SALTASAURUS

➡ A quadrupedal herbivore, small compared to other sauropods

➡ Named for Salta, the area in Argentina where it was first discovered

➡ Was 40 feet long; weighed 20,000 pounds

➡ Had bony plates called osteoderms on its back

FUN FACT *Saltasaurus* was the first sauropod found with osteoderms, the same type of plates found on turtles and crocodiles.

ARGENTINOSAURUS

➡ A quadrupedal herbivore that was the largest land animal ever

➡ Named for Argentina, where it was found by a rancher

➡ Was about 115 feet long; weighed more than 146,000 pounds

➡ A single fossilized vertebra was 6 feet long, the size of a human

FUN FACT An *Argentinosaurus* egg was the size of a coconut—a baby had to grow 25,000 times its hatchling size as it became an adult!

CLEANING FOSSILS

When they are lucky enough to find a fossil, paleontologists take great care not to harm it. Fossils are fragile and may disintegrate when exposed to air. Experts use soft brushes to remove the dirt around a fossil; the dirt is saved so it can be tested. Before a fossil is removed from the soil, experts make sure there are not other fossils around it that could be disturbed.

HYPSELOSAURUS

➡ A quadrupedal herbivore for which few fossils have been found

➡ Name means "high lizard" (*hypsos* means "high" in Greek); originally thought to be a giant crocodile

➡ Was 25–30 feet long; weighed about 20,000 pounds

➡ Had thick, sturdy legs

FUN FACT *Hypselosaurus* is best known for its thin-skinned, foot-long eggs, which were first discovered in France; it was formally named in 1869.

The First Fliers

Experts think there were dinosaurs that flew, such as *Rahonavis*, and there were many other flying prehistoric creatures as well. Fossil evidence gives experts some clues, but few fossils have been found, and there's much more still to discover about how early flight happened.

ARCHAEOPTERYX
Wingspan: 1.5 feet
Late Jurassic period

Archaeopteryx, a theropod dinosaur, is considered by some to be the first bird. It had wings and feathers that would have enabled it to fly. For many years, scientists thought that all birds descended from *Archaeopteryx*, but now they believe that birds descended from other theropods.

ANHANGUERA
Wingspan: 15 feet
Early Cretaceous period

Anhanguera had weak legs and probably spent very little time on the ground.

PTERODACTYLUS
Wingspan: About 3 feet
Late Jurassic period

Like most pterosaurs, *Pterodactylus* had long fingers that were connected to its back legs by a membrane made of skin and muscle. These were its wings, and it flew by flapping its long fingers.

DORYGNATHUS
Wingspan: About 5 feet
Early Jurassic period

Dorygnathus had long, sharp front teeth that it could use to catch and eat fish.

The ability to fly evolved in two groups during the Age of Dinosaurs: flying reptiles called pterosaurs, and birds that descended from theropod dinosaurs.

QUETZALCOATLUS

Wingspan: 35 feet
Late Cretaceous period

Quetzalcoatlus had the largest wingspan of any known animal. It probably pushed off with both front and back legs. Its wings functioned like sails, powering flight.

PTERANODON

Wingspan: 18 feet on adult males, 12 feet on adult females
Late Cretaceous period

Like modern bats, most *Pteranodons* could both fly through the sky and walk on all fours on land.

DID YOU KNOW?

Pterosaurs were large flying reptiles that lived during the Age of Dinosaurs, but they weren't dinosaurs. Until about 50 years ago, some scientists believed that birds evolved from pterosaurs or a close relative, but now all agree that they evolved from theropod dinosaurs.

WHIPTAIL LIZARDS	SIZE	AGE	FOSSILS	LOCATION
Amargasaurus (*uh-**MAR**-guh-sore-us*)	XL	EC	🦴	SA
Amazonsaurus (*a-mah-zon-**SORE**-us*)	XL	EC	🦴	SA
Amphicoelias (*am-fee-**SEE**-lee-iss*)	XXL	LJ	🦴	NA
Apatosaurus (*uh-**PA**-toh-sore-us*)	XXL	LC	🦴	NA
Atlantosaurus (*at-lan-**TOH**-sore-us*)	XXL	LJ	🦴	NA
Barosaurus (*BAH-roh-sore-us*)	XXL	LJ	🦴	AF
Brachytrachelopan (*bra-kee-tra-**CHEH**-lo-pan*)	XL	LJ	🦴	SA
Cathartesaura (*CA-thar-teh-sore-a*)	XXL	LC	🦴	SA
Cetiosauriscus (*SEE-tee-oh-soh-riss-kuss*)	XXL	MJ	🦴	EU
Comahuesaurus (*KO-ma-hoo-SORE-us*)	UN	EC	🦴	SA
Demandasaurus (*duh-**MAN**-do-sore-us*)	L	EC	🦴	EU
Dicraeosaurus (*dy-**CREE**-oh-sore-us*)	XXL	LC	🦴	AF
Dinheirosaurus (*deen-**YAIR**-oh-sore-us*)	XXL	LJ	🦴	NA
Diplodocus (*dih-**PLAH**-duh-kuss*)	XXL	LJ	🦴	NA

	SIZE	AGE	FOSSILS	LOCATION
Dystrophaeus (*dih-stroh-**FEE**-us*)	XL	LJ	🦴	EU
Eocursor (*EE-oh-kur-sore*)	XS	LT	🦴	NA
Haplocanthosaurus (*hap-loh-**KAN**-thoh-sore-us*)	XXL	LJ	🦴	NA
Histriasaurus (*HIH-stree-uh-sore-us*)	M	EC	🦴	AF
Kaatedocus (*cah-teh-**DOH**-kuss*)	XL	LJ	🦴	NA
Leinkupal (*leen-koo-**PAHL***)	XL	EC	🦴	SA
Limaysaurus (*LIH-may-sore-us*)	XXL	MC	🦴	SA
Nigersaurus (*nee-**ZHAIR**-sore-us*)	L	MC	🦴	AF
Rayososaurus (*ray-oh-so-**SORE**-us*)	L	EC	🦴	SA
Rebbachisaurus (*ree-**BA**-sheh-sore-us*)	XXL	LC	🦴	AF/EU
Supersaurus (*SOO-pur-sore-us*)	XXL	LJ	🦴	NA
Suuwassea (*SOO-wah-see-ah*)	XXL	LJ	🦴	NA
Tataouinea (*tah-tah-**WEE**-nee-ah*)	XL	EC	🦴	AF
Tornieria (*TORE-nee-ree-uh*)	XL	LJ	🦴	AF
Zapalasaurus (*zah-**PA**-lah-sore-us*)	XXL	EC	🦴	SA

Nigersaurus

LEGEND

Featured dinosaurs are set in red in the list above.

SIZE
- XS — Under 5 feet
- S — 5-10 feet
- M — 10-20 feet
- L — 20-30 feet
- XL — 30-40 feet
- XXL — Over 40 feet
- UN — Unknown

AGE (years ago)
- LT — Late Triassic (227-201 million)
- EJ — Early Jurassic (201-180 million)
- MJ — Middle Jurassic (180-159 million)
- LJ — Late Jurassic (159-144 million)
- EC — Early Cretaceous (144-98 million)
- LC — Late Cretaceous (98-66 million)

FOSSILS
- Full skeleton
- Partial skeleton
- Skull
- Bone
- Teeth

LOCATION
- AS — Asia
- AF — Africa
- EU — Europe
- AU — Australia
- NA — North America
- SA — South America
- AN — Antarctica

Whiptail Lizards Sauropods

Diplodocus

Whiptail lizards had the body shape that sauropods are known for: very long necks, whiplike tails, and huge torsos with big bellies on short legs. They remind people of dachshunds—but supersize. Some of the biggest and most famous dinosaurs, including *Apatosaurus* and *Diplodocus*, were in the whiptail lizard group. They grew to more than 100 feet long and had some of longest necks and tails ever measured on animals.

Supersize Sauropods

Sauropods are thought to have been the largest animals that ever lived on land; blue whales are bigger, but they are not land animals. The whiptail lizard group included some of the biggest sauropods. *Diplodocus* held the title of biggest dinosaur for a while, but longer sauropods have since been discovered, and new record-breaking fossils are found regularly.

DIPLODOCUS

➡ A quadrupedal herbivore with a small head

➡ Named for a double-beamed bone on the underside of its tail (*diplos* means "double" and *dokos* means "beam" in Greek), which may have helped support its large size

➡ Was up to 108 feet long; weighed about 40,000 pounds

➡ Had a long tail that it could swing around like a whip

FUN FACT A *Diplodocus* skeleton in the Natural History Museum in London has 292 bones and is nicknamed "Dippy."

DR. JOE SAYS

Brachytrachelopan, a very small, short-necked sauropod, throws what we know about sauropods out the window. Paleontologists thought that all sauropods had long necks, but this one is the exception that proves the rule. *Brachytrachelopan* probably ate plants that grew low to the ground, so a short neck worked for it.

— *Dr. Joseph Sertich, Paleontologist*

SUPERSAURUS

➜ A quadrupedal herbivore

➜ Named for its superlarge size

➜ Was up to 112 feet long; weighed about 100,000 pounds

➜ Known for its shoulder blade, the largest single fossilized bone ever found

FUN FACT Bones of a large sauropod originally classified as *Ultrasaurus* were subsequently discovered to be those of *Supersaurus*, and the name *Ultrasaurus* was discarded.

AMARGASAURUS

➜ A quadrupedal herbivore with five toes on each foot

➜ Named for the La Amarga Formation in Argentina, where it was found

➜ Was 33 feet long; weighed 10,000–15,000 pounds

➜ Had blunt teeth for pulling leaves off trees and a big belly for digesting all the plants it ate

FUN FACT *Amargasaurus* had two rows of long, sharp spines on its neck that may have been covered with skin, forming a double sail.

Apatosaurus: Deceptive Lizard

One of the largest animals to have ever lived on land, *Apatosaurus* (originally known as *Brontosaurus*) is also one of the most recognizable and popular dinosaurs of all time. It was very strong and heavily built, with vertebrae arranged in such a way that it was able to hold its tail above the ground to maintain balance. Its name, which means "deceptive lizard," was chosen by O. C. Marsh because some of its bones were similar to those of non-dinosaur marine reptiles. The earlier name, *Brontosaurus*, means "thunder lizard"; the heavy steps of this huge animal would have made a sound like thunder.

SO BIG!

Sauropods include some of the biggest creatures that ever lived. Usually, size is measured by head-to-tail length, but sauropods had other huge features as well.

Tail length
Diplodocus,
45 feet long

Height
Sauroposeidon,
60 feet tall

HEADS WILL ROLL

For about 100 years, the dinosaur that is now known as *Apatosaurus* was called *Brontosaurus*. Why was the name changed? O. C. Marsh discovered two dinosaur skeletons in the late nineteenth century. He named the first one *Apatosaurus* and the second one *Brontosaurus*. Neither skeleton had its head attached; sauropod skulls are lightly attached to their bodies and often roll away. For a while scientists thought they had two different dinosaurs, with heads belonging to other dinosaurs even finding their way onto one or the other skeleton. Later, paleontologists studying the bones closely recognized that they were the same animal and the first name given, *Apatosaurus*, is the one that is now used.

SAURUS STORY

PALEO DATA

APATOSAURUS

PRONUNCIATION
uh-PA-toh-sore-us

SIZE
70–90 feet long; weighed 70,000–80,000 pounds

AGE
Late Jurassic, about 150 million years ago

LOCATION
Western United States

FOSSILS
Several partial skeletons

DIET
Plants

Weight
Brachiosaurus,
160,000 pounds

Neck length
Mamenchisaurus,
32 feet long

Single bone size
Supersaurus vertebra, 8 feet

Survival Tactics

Dinosaurs had a number of skills and body parts they could use in a fight. They used their senses—sight, hearing, smell—to detect prey or predators. Many could run quickly, which was good for chasing or escaping. And their bodies were equipped with built-in tools for survival.

ATTACK TOOLS FOR CARNIVORES

Meat-eating dinosaurs used many skills and strategies when on the attack.

Tyrannosaurus rex

SHARP TEETH AND CLAWS Big meat eaters had lots of large, sharp, curved teeth in their jaws. Some of the teeth were serrated like steak knives. Even toothless theropods had lethal claws on their hands and feet that could catch and rip apart prey.

Carcharodontosaurus attacks a young Paralititan.

STRENGTH Jaws and beaks on meat-eating dinosaurs were strong, and big carnivores could bite with tremendous strength. Birdlike theropods had hard beaks and bills that could crush small reptiles and shellfish.

Skorpiovenator devours an Argentinosaurus hatchling.

PICKING OFF THE WEAK Dinosaurs chose their battles. They targeted young and wounded prey that they knew they could kill. Even the biggest predators were likely also scavengers—they would eat something that was already dead rather than pick a fight.

Sinornithosaurus attack Jeholosaurus.

ATTACKING IN PACKS Alone, even the biggest carnivore—such as a Giganotosaurus or a Spinosaurus, each 50 feet long—was no match for a 100-foot-long sauropod. Carnivores may have hunted in packs; three or four of them could overpower a big sauropod and then share the meat.

A dinosaur's life wasn't easy. They often had to fight to stay alive, both because they needed to kill in order to have food to eat and because they needed to defend themselves from predators.

DEFENSE TOOLS FOR HERBIVORES

Gentle herbivores had no reason to attack, but they needed fighting tools and strategies to avoid being eaten.

Diplodocus

SIZE By the Late Cretaceous period, the biggest herbivores, such as *Diplodocus*, were more than 100 feet long. With height, length, and weight on their side, they could disarm a 40-foot carnivore by stepping on it or whipping it with a superlong tail.

Parasaurolophus

SPEED The biggest herbivores couldn't run very fast, but smaller ones, such as *Parasaurolophus*, could rear up on two legs and run away at more than 30 miles per hour, faster than the biggest carnivores could pursue.

A *Miragaia* herd defends itself from *Torvosaurus*.

STICKING TOGETHER Often traveling in herds, herbivores could fend off attacks by circling their young to keep them safe. If attacked by a pack, several herbivores could fight back using horns, whiplike tails, and giant, stomping feet.

Triceratops

BODY ARMOR Herbivores developed amazing body armor. *Triceratops* had big, sharp horns on its head. *Stegosaurus* had sharp projections up and down its spine.

Some dinosaur skeletons have been found locked in battle. Others have been found with scars on the bones, giving clues as to which dinosaurs fought one another. The scenes below tell stories, based on facts, of what might have happened when these dinosaurs did battle.

ON THE SCENE

T. REX VS. TRICERATOPS

T. REX:
➡ Up to 40 feet long; weighed 18,000 pounds
➡ Huge, banana-shaped teeth; massive jaw
➡ Carnivore

TRICERATOPS:
➡ Up to 25 feet long; weighed 12,000 pounds
➡ Three sharp horns on its head
➡ Herbivore

Triceratops grazes in a clearing. Suddenly it senses danger. A huge *Tyrannosaurus rex* has emerged from the forest and looms above *Triceratops*. *T. rex* makes its move. *Triceratops* defends itself by pushing its sharp horns into the predator's side, drawing blood. The carnivore has size in its favor, though, and sinks 8-inch-long teeth into the herbivore's back. *Triceratops* swings around to avoid another bite from *T. rex*'s massive jaws; using its bony frill and solid skull, it knocks the larger dinosaur off balance. Again and again, horns pierce flesh, until *T. rex* falls over. As the carnivore lies bleeding on the ground, *Triceratops* walks away to nurse its wounds.

This battle actually took place. Two skeletons, of a *Velociraptor* and a *Protoceratops*, were found in the Gobi desert, locked in battle with limbs intertwined. Scientists think that the two were fighting when a sandstorm killed them both.

ON THE SCENE

VELOCIRAPTOR VS. PROTOCERATOPS

VELOCIRAPTOR:
➜ Up to 6½ feet long; weighed 40 pounds
➜ Small, sharp teeth; big, sharp claws
➜ Carnivore

PROTOCERATOPS:
➜ Up to 6 feet long; weighed 400 pounds
➜ Small frill on its head; hard beak
➜ Herbivore

It's twilight, and *Protoceratops* has just finished a long day of munching grass when a quick *Velociraptor* swoops in. Both dinosaurs can see well in the fading light, but only *Velociraptor* has sharp claws. *Velociraptor* is not interested in the heavy herbivore; it is moving toward the eggs that *Protoceratops* has been guarding. *Protoceratops* gets between the nest and the predator. Out come the sharp claws, to do their damage. *Protoceratops* clings to the lighter animal, but it cannot inflict pain with its toothless beak and flimsy frill. *Velociraptor* keeps swinging its claws until the herbivore stops moving; it grabs the eggs from the nest and leaves the scene.

At the beginning of the Early Jurassic period, after dinosaurs had split into bird-hipped and lizard-hipped orders, they evolved at an increasingly rapid pace. Thyreophorans were among the earliest dinosaurs of this period. They were heavy, slow-moving quadrupedal herbivores, ranging from just a few feet to almost 40 feet in length. They had small heads that held tiny brains; their brain-to-body-size ratio was the smallest of all dinosaurs.

Thyreophorans had impressive protective body armor. There were two main types: stegosaurs had triangular bony plates running along their backs, and ankylosaurs were covered in fused, or connected, bony plates that sometimes had spikes jutting out.

▷ Its barbed tail could be used as a weapon.

Stegosaurus

LATE TRIASSIC

227 TO 201
MILLION YEARS AGO

Ornithischians first appeared; this group included thyreophorans, ornithopods, and marginocephalians.

EARLY JURASSIC

201 TO 180
MILLION YEARS AGO

Scutellosaurus, a small North American dinosaur with light armor, was the first thyreophoran.

MIDDLE JURASSIC

180 TO 159
MILLION YEARS AGO

Scelidosaurus developed heavier armor, though not as heavy as the armor of later thyreophorans.

Thyreophorans

▶ The bony plates along its spine may have helped *Stegosaurus* attract a mate.

AT A GLANCE

The name *thyreophoran* comes from Greek and means "shield bearer." It refers to the bony coverings this group had on their bodies. Thyreophoran fossils have been found on all seven continents, but they are most common in the western United States. There are 80 known thyreophorans.

Thyreophorans were:
➡ part of the ornithischian (bird-hipped) order of dinosaurs
➡ quadrupedal
➡ herbivores

Thyreophorans are divided into two sections in this book:

Shield Bearers
➡ Ranged from small, primitive dinosaurs with little armor to large, heavily armored dinosaurs
➡ Had triangular bony plates down their spines
➡ Many had barbed tails used for defense

Armored Lizards
➡ Were covered in tightly connected plates
➡ Had tails that ended in bony clubs

Some well-known thyreophorans: *Stegosaurus, Ankylosaurus, Kentrosaurus*

LATE JURASSIC

159 TO 144
MILLION YEARS AGO

Stegosaurs, with clubbed tails and triangular plates on their spines, roamed Earth.

EARLY CRETACEOUS

144 TO 98
MILLION YEARS AGO

Nodosaurs, early versions of ankylosaurs, appeared. They had fused plates but no clubbed tails.

LATE CRETACEOUS

98 TO 66
MILLION YEARS AGO

Ankylosaurs, which had heavy armor, lived until the end of this period, when all dinosaurs vanished.

EARLY ORNITHISCHIANS AND HETERODONTOSAURS

	SIZE	AGE	FOSSILS	LOCATION
Abrictosaurus (*uh-**BRIK**-toh-sore-us*)	XS	MJ	Skull/Partial skeleton	AS
Echinodon (*ee-**KY**-noh-don*)	XS	LJ	Partial skeleton/Bone	EU
Fruitadens (***FROO**-tah-dens*)	XS	LJ	Skull/Partial skeleton/Bone	NA
Heterodontosaurus (*heh-tur-oh-**DON**-toe-sore-us*)	XS	EJ	Partial skeleton/Bone	AF
Lycorhinus (*ly-koh-**RY**-nus*)	S	EJ	Teeth/Skull	AF
Pisanosaurus (*pee-**ZAH**-no-sore-us*)	XS	LT	Partial skeleton/Bone	SA
Tianyulong (*tee-ahn-**YOO**-long*)	XS	EC	Skull/Partial skeleton/Bone	AS

BASAL THYREOPHORANS

	SIZE	AGE	FOSSILS	LOCATION
Bienosaurus (***BEE**-en-oh-sore-us*)	S	EJ	Skull	AS
Emausaurus (***EE**-mauh-sore-us*)	S	EJ	Skull/Bone	EU
Scelidosaurus (***SKEL**-eye-doh-sore-us*)	M	EJ	Full skeleton/Bone	NA/EU
Scutellosaurus (*skoo-**TEH**-loh-sore-us*)	XS	EJ	Partial skeleton/Bone	NA
Tatisaurus (*tah-tee-**SORE**-us*)	XS	EJ	Bone	AS

STEGOSAURS

	SIZE	AGE	FOSSILS	LOCATION
Chialingosaurus (*chee-uh-ling-oh-**SORE**-us*)	M	MJ	Partial skeleton/Bone	AS
Chungkingosaurus (*chung-king-oh-**SORE**-us*)	M	LJ	Partial skeleton/Bone	AS
Dacentrurus (*dah-sen-**TROO**-russ*)	M	LJ	Partial skeleton/Bone	EU
Gigantspinosaurus (***JY**-gant-spy-noh-sore-us*)	M	LJ	Partial skeleton/Bone	AS
Huayangosaurus (*hwah-yang-oh-**SORE**-us*)	M	MJ	Full skeleton/Bone	AS
Jiangjunosaurus (***JEE**-ang-joo-noh-sore-us*)	L	LJ	Skull/Partial skeleton/Bone	AS
Kentrosaurus (***KEN**-troh-**SORE**-us*)	M	LJ	Partial skeleton/Bone	AF
Lexovisaurus (***LEX**-oh-vee-sore-us*)	M	MJ	Bone	EU
Miragaia (***MEE**-rah-gai-ah*)	L	LJ	Skull/Partial skeleton/Bone	EU
Monkonosaurus (*mong-**KAHN**-uh-sore-us*)	M	LC	Partial skeleton/Bone	AS
Paranthodon (*pa-**RAN**-thoh-don*)	M	LJ	Skull	AF
Regnosaurus (*reg-no-**SORE**-us*)	M	EC	Bone	EU
Stegosaurus (***STEH**-go-sore-us*)	L	LJ	Full skeleton/Bone	NA
Tuojiangosaurus (*too-oh-gee-**ANG**-go-sore-us*)	L	LJ	Partial skeleton/Bone	AS
Wuerhosaurus (*woo-**AIR**-hoh-sore-us*)	L	EC	Partial skeleton/Bone	AS

Scelidosaurus

LEGEND

Featured dinosaurs are set in red in the list above.

SIZE
XS	Under 5 feet
S	5-10 feet
M	10-20 feet
L	20-30 feet
XL	30-40 feet
XXL	Over 40 feet
UN	Unknown

AGE (years ago)
LT	Late Triassic (227-201 million)
EJ	Early Jurassic (201-180 million)
MJ	Middle Jurassic (180-159 million)
LJ	Late Jurassic (159-144 million)
EC	Early Cretaceous (144-98 million)
LC	Late Cretaceous (98-66 million)

FOSSILS
	Full skeleton
	Partial skeleton
	Skull
	Bone
	Teeth

LOCATION
AS	Asia
AF	Africa
EU	Europe
AU	Australia
NA	North America
SA	South America
AN	Antarctica

Shield Bearers Thyreophorans
Early Ornithischians to Stegosaurs

What set shield bearers such as *Stegosaurus* and *Gigantspinosaurus*, also known as stegosaurs, apart was their body armor. Pointy, triangular plates ran along thyreophorans' spines; some of them also had sharp spikes sticking out of their bodies. These plates and spikes made them less attractive to predators, since sharp teeth couldn't crush them. Stegosaurs also had hard beaks that they used to snip leaves and twigs off low-growing plants.

Dacentrurus

Thyreophorans had hard, horny beaks that could clip leaves and twigs from trees, which allowed them to gather food quickly. Their striking spinal triangles weren't used as weapons; experts think they were used as a display to identify themselves to other members of the group. Their spiked tails, however, were excellent defensive weapons.

GIGANTSPINOSAURUS

➤ A quadrupedal herbivore, for which a nearly complete skeleton was found in China

➤ Named for the two gigantic spines, or spikes, that stuck out of its shoulders

➤ Was 15 feet long; weighed about 2,000 pounds

➤ Had ridged skin covered in evenly spaced scales

FUN FACT At first, it was thought that *Gigantspinosaurus*'s spikes stuck out of its hips; in 2006, experts realized they had been positioned upside down by mistake and actually fit on the shoulders.

BUILT-IN WEAPONS

Thyreophorans had many body parts that served as defense weapons to help them survive.

Scuttelosaurus
Fused plates

Huayangosaurus
Triangular plates

Gastonia
Spikes

Dacentrurus
Barbed tail

Ankylosaurus
Clubbed tail

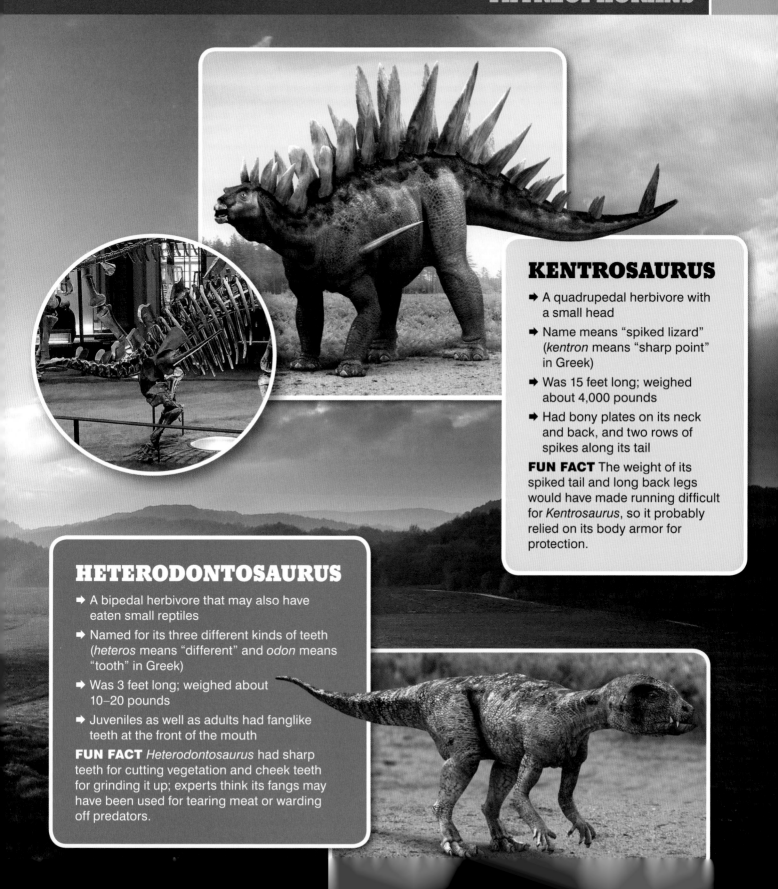

KENTROSAURUS

➡ A quadrupedal herbivore with a small head

➡ Name means "spiked lizard" (*kentron* means "sharp point" in Greek)

➡ Was 15 feet long; weighed about 4,000 pounds

➡ Had bony plates on its neck and back, and two rows of spikes along its tail

FUN FACT The weight of its spiked tail and long back legs would have made running difficult for *Kentrosaurus*, so it probably relied on its body armor for protection.

HETERODONTOSAURUS

➡ A bipedal herbivore that may also have eaten small reptiles

➡ Named for its three different kinds of teeth (*heteros* means "different" and *odon* means "tooth" in Greek)

➡ Was 3 feet long; weighed about 10–20 pounds

➡ Juveniles as well as adults had fanglike teeth at the front of the mouth

FUN FACT *Heterodontosaurus* had sharp teeth for cutting vegetation and cheek teeth for grinding it up; experts think its fangs may have been used for tearing meat or warding off predators.

When a dinosaur had hard, pointy plates up and down its back, predators weren't likely to eat it. Bony triangles attached to *Stegosaurus*'s skin helped it survive—an important defense for a dinosaur that moved slowly and wasn't very aggressive. *Stegosaurus* was an herbivore, walked on four legs, and had a tiny brain. At up to 40 feet long, it was about ten times the size of a dog, but its brain was only one-quarter the size of a dog's brain.

TALE OF A TAIL

Stegosaurus and many of its relatives have an interesting tail feature: four spikes arranged in a pattern. Paleontologists have done tests with models of these spikes that show that a tail with this feature would have been an effective weapon if swung hard at an attacker. *Stegosaurus* had the muscles to do damage using its tail as a barbed club.

PALEO DATA

STEGOSAURUS

PRONUNCIATION
STEH-go-sore-us

SIZE
25–40 feet long; weighed 7,000 pounds

AGE
Late Jurassic, about 150 million years ago

LOCATION
Western United States

FOSSILS
Several partial and complete skeletons

DIET
Plants

WHEN IS A TURTLE NOT A TURTLE?

When paleontologist O. C. Marsh first found a *Stegosaurus* skeleton in the 1870s, he couldn't figure out where the bony plates fit. He thought that he had found the skeleton of a giant turtle, and that the plates covered the turtle's shell. With more study, he thought the plates extended only from the tail. Another theory was that the plates covered the dinosaur's body like shingles on a roof, so *Stegosaurus* has sometimes been called the shingled dinosaur—its scientific name means "roof lizard." Later, when a more complete skeleton was found, experts could see how the plates were arranged on the dinosaur's back.

HERD MENTALITY

Track marks indicate that *Stegosaurus* and its relatives may have lived in herds. Living in herds would have helped them protect their young, which were born without protective bony plates.

Birth of a Dinosaur

While all evidence has pointed to the fact that dinosaurs hatched from eggs laid by females, this was not confirmed until about 100 years ago. There now have been many exciting discoveries of eggs and nests of different species so the hatching of dinosaur babies from eggs is now accepted.

NESTING *Eoraptor* males showed the nests they built to females. This was part of a mating ritual.

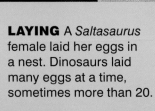

LAYING A *Saltasaurus* female laid her eggs in a nest. Dinosaurs laid many eggs at a time, sometimes more than 20.

BROODING
Like modern birds, many dinosaur mothers, including troodontids and *Gigantoraptor* (left), sat on their nests to keep their eggs warm at night and cool during the day until they hatched. This process, called brooding, ensures that eggs have a steady source of heat to develop properly.

Even the biggest, deadliest dinosaur started out as a baby hatched from an egg. Fossils of young and adult dinosaurs have been found in groups; from these fossil groups, scientists have learned a great deal about how dinosaur babies were born and grew.

CRRR-ACK

What happened to the baby dinosaurs after they cracked through their shells? By studying fossilized leg bones of baby dinosaurs, experts can tell that some dinosaurs, including *Argentinosaurus*, were able to take care of themselves as soon as they were born.

DINOSAUR EGGS

Dinosaur eggs were large, but smaller than one would expect from animals that could grow to 100 feet long. The largest dinosaur eggs were only about 18 inches long—which means that even the most gigantic dinosaurs had small babies.

EUREKA!

In 1978, paleontologist John "Jack" Horner made an incredible discovery of fossilized dinosaur nests, eggshells, and embryos in Montana—the first dinosaur eggs found in the Weastern Hemisphere! From this important find, we learned a lot: how dinosaurs made their nests, cared for their eggs, and fed their babies after they were hatched.

Growing Up

Many dinosaurs went through a period of infancy, like human babies do, when their parents took care of all their needs. That was followed by a childhood, when they learned to move around, find food, and avoid attack. Dinosaurs grew slowly for the first few years of their lives—and then grew amazingly large, amazingly quickly.

LEARNING

Young dinosaurs learned how to find food by hunting or foraging (finding plant food) with their parents. These parents browsed with their young and protected them when predators came near.

Herd of *Argentinosaurus*

HOW LONG DID DINOSAURS LIVE?

Based on the fossils that have been found, old age was not the cause of death for most dinosaurs. A dinosaur had to survive harsh climates—with storms and floods—volcanoes, and predators. It had to find enough food to keep from starving. Even though researchers don't have many skeletons to test for age, they have made some educated guesses based on similar modern animals and growth rings that appear in bones. Gigantic herbivorous dinosaurs, such as *Apatosaurus* and *Diplodocus*, lived for 70 to 80 years, while big carnivores lived only 30 to 40 years.

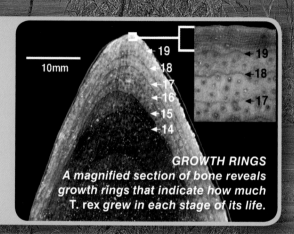

10mm

GROWTH RINGS
A magnified section of bone reveals growth rings that indicate how much T. rex grew in each stage of its life.

FAMILY MATTERS

Dinosaur parents protected their young, before and after they hatched. Young dinosaurs often stayed in their nests for more than just a few weeks or months, and even after they left the nest, dinosaurs hung around with their siblings. Here are a few examples showing dinosaur family behavior:

▶ A nest found in Mongolia showed 15 *Protoceratops* that were each about 5 feet long; researchers estimate that they were one year old and still being cared for by their parents.

▶ Fossil finds of young dinosaurs with both male and female adults suggest that dinosaur fathers may have stayed around to care for their young.

▶ At Como Bluff, Wyoming, 20 adult and young *Drinker* dinosaurs were found together in a burrow, with the adults on top of the children. Scientists think that the parents pushed their children into the burrow to escape a predator.

GROWTH RATES

By the time it reached the age of ten, a *Tyrannosaurus rex* weighed about 1,000 pounds.

In the next few years, it grew half a ton each year until it reached its adult weight of 12,000 pounds.

After that, when it was able to reproduce and therefore considered adult, it grew very little.

DINO DETAILS
53 ARMORED LIZARDS THYREOPHORANS

POLACANTHUS AND ITS RELATIVES

	SIZE	AGE	FOSSILS	LOCATION
Dongyangopelta (*DONG*-yang-oh-pel-*tah*)	UN	EC	Bone	AS
Gargoyleosaurus (*GAR*-goil-oh-sore-*us*)	S	LJ	Full skeleton	NA
Gastonia (gas-*TOE*-nee-uh)	M	EC	Full skeleton	NA
Hoplitosaurus (hoh-*PLEE*-toh-sore-us)	M	EC	Partial skeleton	NA
Hylaeosaurus (hy-*LEE*-oh-sore-us)	M	EC	Full skeleton	EU
Mymoorapelta (mee-*MOH*-rah-pel-tah)	S	LJ	Skull, Partial skeleton	NA
Polacanthus (pol-uh-*KAN*-thuss)	M	EC	Partial skeleton	EU
Taohelong (dow-hoo-*WUHR*-long)	UN	EC	Bone	AS
Zhejiangosaurus (dzie-*JEE*-yang-oh-sore-us)	M	EC	Partial skeleton	AS

NODOSAURS

	SIZE	AGE	FOSSILS	LOCATION
Aletopelta (al-ee-toe-*PEL*-tah)	M	LC	Partial skeleton	NA
Animantarx (ann-ee-*MAN*-tarks)	S	LC	Skull, Partial skeleton	NA
Anoplosaurus (an-*OP*-loh-sore-us)	UN	EC	Partial skeleton	EU
Antarctopelta (an-tark-toe-*PEL*-tah)	M	LC	Skull, Partial skeleton	AN
Denversaurus (*DEN*-vur-sore-us)	M	LC	Skull	NA
Edmontonia (ed-mon-*TONE*-ee-uh)	L	LC	Skull	NA
Europelta (yoor-oh-*PEL*-tah)	M	EC	Partial skeleton	EU
Glyptodontopelta (glip-toe-dahnt-oh-*PEL*-tah)	M	LC	Bone	NA
Hungarosaurus (*HUN*-gair-oh-sore-us)	M	LC	Full skeleton	EU
Niobrarasaurus (nee-oh-*BRAH*-ruh-sore-us)	M	LC	Skull	NA
Nodosaurus (*NO*-doh-sore-us)	M	EC	Partial skeleton	NA
Panoplosaurus (*PA*-noh-ploh-sore-us)	L	LC	Skull, Partial skeleton	NA
Pawpawsaurus (paw-paw-*SORE*-us)	M	LC	Skull	NA
Peloroplites (peh-lor-oh-*PLEE*-teez)	M	EC	Skull, Partial skeleton	NA
Propanoplosaurus (pro-pan-oh-ploh-*SORE*-us)	UN	EC	Bone	NA
Sauropelta (sore-oh-*PEL*-tah)	L	EC	Partial skeleton	NA
Silvisaurus (sill-*vih*-*SORE*-us)	M	EC	Bone	NA
Stegopelta (STEG-o-*PEL*-tah)	L	EC	Partial skeleton	NA
Struthiosaurus (stroo-theeh-oh-*SORE*-us)	S	LC	Partial skeleton	EU
Tatankacephalus (tah-tank-uh-*SEFF*-a-luss)	M	EC	Teeth, Skull, Partial skeleton	NA
Texasetes (tek-sa-*SEE*-teez)	M	LC	Teeth, Skull, Partial skeleton	NA

ANKYLOSAURS

	SIZE	AGE	FOSSILS	LOCATION
Ahshislepelta (ah-shi-sleh-*PEL*-tah)	S	LC	Partial skeleton	NA
Ankylosaurus (an-ky-loh-*SORE*-us)	L	LC	Skull, Partial skeleton	NA
Anodontosaurus (an-oh-*DAHNT*-oh-sore-us)	M	LC	Full skeleton	NA
Cedarpelta (see-dar-*PEL*-tah)	L	EC	Skull	NA
Crichtonsaurus (*CRY*-ton-sore-us)	S	LC	Skull, Full skeleton, Partial skeleton	AS
Dyoplosaurus (*DY*-oh-ploh-sore-us)	L	LC	Bone	NA
Euoplocephalus (*YOU*-oh-ploh-seff-uh-luss)	L	LC	Full skeleton	NA
Gobisaurus (go-bee-*SORE*-us)	L	EC	Skull	AS
Liaoningosaurus (*LEE*-ow-ning-oh-sore-us)	XS	EC	Full skeleton	AS
Minmi (*MIN*-mee)	S	EC	Full skeleton	AU
Minotaurasaurus (*MIH*-no-tar-uh-sore-us)	S	LC	Skull	AS
Nodocephalosaurus (no-doh-*SEFF*-uh-loh-sore-us)	M	LC	Skull	NA
Oohkotokia (oo-oh-koh-*TOKE*-ee-uh)	M	LC	Skull, Partial skeleton	NA
Pinacosaurus (*PIN*-uh-coh-sore-us)	M	LC	Partial skeleton	AS
Saichania (sy-*CHAY*-nee-uh)	L	LC	Full skeleton	AS
Scolosaurus (*SKOH*-loh-sore-us)	M	LC	Partial skeleton	NA
Shamosaurus (sha-moh-*SORE*-us)	L	EC	Partial skeleton	AS
Shanxia (shan-*SHEE*-ah)	M	LC	Partial skeleton	AS
Talarurus (tal-uh-*ROO*-rus)	M	LC	Full skeleton	AS
Tarchia (*TAHR*-key-uh)	L	LC	Full skeleton	AS
Tianzhenosaurus (tee-en-shen-oh-*SORE*-us)	M	EC	Full skeleton	AS
Tsagantegia (*SAH*-gan-teh-gee-uh)	L	EC	Skull	AS
Zhongyuansaurus (jong-*YOO*-an-sore-us)	S	EC	Skull, Partial skeleton	AS

LEGEND

Featured dinosaurs are set in red in the list above.

SIZE
- XS — Under 5 feet
- S — 5-10 feet
- M — 10-20 feet
- L — 20-30 feet
- XL — 30-40 feet
- XXL — Over 40 feet
- UN — Unknown

AGE (years ago)
- LT — Late Triassic (227-201 million)
- EJ — Early Jurassic (201-180 million)
- MJ — Middle Jurassic (180-159 million)
- LJ — Late Jurassic (159-144 million)
- EC — Early Cretaceous (144-98 million)
- LC — Late Cretaceous (98-66 million)

FOSSILS
- Full skeleton
- Partial skeleton
- Skull
- Bone
- Teeth

LOCATION
- AS — Asia
- AF — Africa
- EU — Europe
- AU — Australia
- NA — North America
- SA — South America
- AN — Antarctica

Armored Lizards Thyreophorans

Built like tanks, armored lizards had fused bony plates all over their bodies. The earliest species, such as *Polacanthus* and *Nodosaurus*, were covered in light plates and thin spikes. By the time ankylosaurs appeared in the Early Cretaceous period, this group had thick protective armor made of fused bones with pointy spikes sticking up between the bones. Their bodies had become a valuable tool, protecting them from predators.

Struthiosaurus

Built Like Tanks

Although they appear similar at first glance, each member of this group had a different arrangement of body armor. All were quadrupedal herbivores with small heads and short legs.

NODOSAURUS

➡ A quadrupedal herbivore that was small and slow

➡ Named for the nodes, or knobs, all over its body

➡ Was about 15 feet long; weighed 1,000–2,000 pounds

➡ Had no club on its tail or other defensive weapon

FUN FACT *Nodosaurus*'s knobby body was a bunker, but it had a soft belly. It may have dropped down and hugged the ground to protect itself when attacked.

MINMI

➡ A quadrupedal herbivore, as the first thyreophoran found in the Southern Hemisphere

➡ Named for Minmi Crossing in Queensland, Australia, near where it was found

➡ Was 6–10 feet long; weighed about 500–700 pounds

➡ Had spikes, plates, and ossicles (small bones) all over its body and tail

FUN FACT *Minmi* was a nibbler that bit off tiny parts of plants rather than swallowing them whole (small bits of plants were found in the stomach of a well-preserved fossil).

EUOPLOCEPHALUS

➔ A quadrupedal herbivore found in western Canada
➔ Name means "well-armored head" in Greek
➔ Was 20 feet long; weighed 4,000 pounds
➔ Had a triangle-shaped skull with a snout that drooped down

FUN FACT Fossilized *Euoplocephalus* tracks show that this short-legged dinosaur could move quickly.

WORD

Browsing, for an herbivore, means eating small plants, leaves, and fruits from woody plants like shrubs. There was no grass for grazing at this time, so these dinosaurs ate by browsing.

SAUROPELTA

➔ A quadrupedal herbivore that is one of the best-known armored dinosaurs
➔ Name means "lizard shield" in Greek
➔ Was 25 feet long; weighed 3,000–3,500 pounds
➔ Had a small head and a narrow, sharp beak perfect for munching on low shrubs

FUN FACT *Sauropelta* lived in the western United States, in an area covered by forests.

FOSSIL FILE

Fossilized *Ankylosaurus* jaws show wear in the joints, indicating that the jaws moved back and forth as it chewed its food. This helped it digest food quickly and take in enough nourishment to support its big, heavy body.

Ankylosaurus had a very heavy body on short, thick legs. It wasn't able to rear up on its hind legs to eat from the tops of trees. The heavy armor that surrounded its body would have made it unattractive to predators—even big, sharp teeth couldn't pierce the tanklike covering. *Ankylosaurus* weighed more than 8,000 pounds when fully grown; even the biggest carnivore would not have been able to tip it over to get to its soft underbelly.

WICKED WAGGING

The club at the end of a young *Ankylosaurus* was about as big and heavy as a bowling ball. As the dinosaur grew up, the club grew bigger. A hard thwack from that kind of tail could have broken the bones of a predator that dared to attack it.

DEFENSIVE ARMOR

Body armor isn't unique to dinosaurs. Many modern animals also have body armor of one sort or another.

Sharp Quills
Porcupines are covered in sharp quills that they can shoot at animals when threatened or attacked

Bony Plates
Armadillos are sheathed in bands of bony plates made of scales encased in bone. This tough exterior protects

DID YOU KNOW?

Ankylosaurus fossils have been dated from about 66 million years ago. It was one of the last dinosaurs to appear, and it lived right up to the time when all dinosaurs became extinct.

PALEO DATA

ANKYLOSAURUS

PRONUNCIATION
an-ky-loh-**SORE**-us

SIZE
25–35 feet long; weighed 6,000-8,000 pounds

AGE
Late Cretaceous, about 66 million years ago

LOCATION
Western United States and Canada

FOSSILS
Several partial skeletons

DIET
Plants

Scutes
A tortoise is protected by its upper and lower shells. The upper shell is layered with scales called scutes.

Abandoned Shells
Soft-bodied hermit crabs hide in hard shells discarded by other creatures. As they grow bigger, they need to find bigger shells to inhabit.

Leathery Hide
The Indian rhinoceros is covered in thick, leathery hide that protects it from both the elements and attackers.

Dispatches From a Dig

Dr. Joe Sertich and a team of paleontologists had made numerous discoveries on the island of Madagascar over a period of 20 years, so when they heard rumors of dinosaur bones on a different part of the island, in much older rocks, they knew they had to mount an expedition. Learn all about it in Dr. Joe's report of the new discovery.

1 PREPARATION

First, we assembled a group of scientists to look into background information on the new area, including its geology and history of exploration. We teamed up with paleontologists and paleontology students from the University of Antananarivo in Madagascar, then gathered the equipment we would need to bring with us to help excavate a new dinosaur: special glues, specimen bags, and a saw to cut through hard rock.

2 TRAVEL

Our long journey took us through London, England, and Nairobi, Kenya, on our way to Antananarivo, the capital of Madagascar. We had dinner with friends and colleagues on our first night in Madagascar. Everyone was eager to get to the field, but dead tired from all the travel.

3 OUR TEAM

By the time we reached camp, our team consisted of nearly 20 people: two professional drivers, three paleontology students from Madagascar, a geologist, a paleobotanist, and two dinosaur paleontologists, including myself—plus local guides and helpers from the surrounding community.

4 GEARING UP

Gathering what we needed for the dig

We needed gear for our mission and supplies for our team. Over the next several days, we scrambled to find 4,000 pounds of plaster and burlap for jacketing specimens, along with the necessary food for the four weeks of work. We camped in tents for the entire trip, with our water coming from creeks and rivers.

5 FINDING OUR WAY

The dinosaur discovery site was a three-day drive from the big city of Antananarivo, with the final 10 miles off road through dry grasslands. A local guide directed the cars through chest-high grass and around obstacles like rocks, trees, and holes so big that they could swallow an entire truck. We made it to our campsite just as the sun was setting. As we drifted off to sleep, small mouse lemurs scurried through the branches above our heads.

Crossing the river

6 DISCOVERY

As we crested the hill and walked through the tall grass toward the site, I was doubtful that anyone could have found fossils in such a remote location. Then—there it was! We could tell that we were seeing an amazing thing: Exposed on the surface were at least 20 tail vertebrae and part of the femur of a huge titanosaur sauropod.

Me, with the partial femur of a huge titanosaur

7 EXCAVATION

Fortunately, the dinosaur was just below the surface of the grass. As we removed the soil, we revealed a fully articulated tail and the hind leg of a HUGE sauropod. We spent every day, from sunrise to sunset, excavating huge sections of the skeleton from the ground. We moved quickly to protect the fossils, encasing each section in a plaster-of-paris field jacket. Each weighed between 200 and 1,000 pounds.

Wrapping fossil sections in plaster-of-paris field jackets

Moving a heavy fossil section

8 TRANSPORTATION

Moving a mega dino from the field site is not an easy task. We loaded all the encased fossils onto oxcarts for the journey across the roadless countryside. They were then transferred to a massive truck for transport back to Antananarivo. From there they were inspected, were transported to the coast, crossed the Atlantic Ocean on a ship, and traveled by truck across the United States to Denver. This took nearly two years!

Securing a fossil section to an ox-cart

9 RESEARCH BEGINS

Finally, the fossils arrived at the Denver Museum of Nature & Science. There is much to do before we can begin studying the fossils, and I will need to be patient over the next year or two as the plaster and rock are carefully removed from the 50 bones we collected. I suspect that they represent a new species of titanosaur sauropod dinosaur—I can't wait to find out!

DINO DETECTIVE

STUDYING A NEW FOSSIL

When a newly discovered fossil is finally at the lab, a paleontologist studies it in many ways. It is examined under a magnifying glass to see if it has any diseases or breaks. It is compared to similar bones to see if the genus of the animal it came from can be identified. The next step is to match it to other similar bones to see where it fits into a dinosaur's body.

Ornithopods are not the best-known dinosaurs; there is no famous ornithopod that everyone recognizes, even though it's a large group with 130 known species. Ornithopods were successful, though. They grew in both population and size, with the help of a very useful ability: They were good at chewing. Their teeth and digestive systems allowed them to process food in both their mouths and their stomachs, much like cows and sheep do today, to extract nutrients they needed to thrive.

Dinosaurs in this group are known for other features as well: Some had duckbills for snipping off vegetation; some had thumbs that stuck out sideways and could be used to ward off predators and gather food; and most could walk on either four feet or two feet, depending on whether they were browsing or running.

▶ Back legs were longer than front legs, giving it a bent posture.

LATE TRIASSIC	EARLY JURASSIC	MIDDLE JURASSIC
227 TO 201 **MILLION YEARS AGO** No ornithopod fossils have been found from this period yet.	**201 TO 180** **MILLION YEARS AGO** No ornithopod fossils have been found from this period yet.	**180 TO 159** **MILLION YEARS AGO** The earliest ornithopods, *Thescelosaurus* and *Dryosaurus*, appeared; they were bipedal. They were small—some only 10 feet long—but very fast.

Ornithopods

Camptosaurus

▶ Three-toed feet were good for running fast to escape predators.

AT A GLANCE

The name *ornithopod* comes from a Greek word meaning "bird feet"—most of these dinosaurs had three-toed feet that looked like those of birds of today. Ornithopod fossils have been found on all seven continents, but most ornithopods lived in the Northern Hemisphere. There are 130 known ornithopods.

Ornithopods were:
➡ part of the ornithischian (bird-hipped) order of dinosaurs
➡ quadrupedal: they walked on four feet while browsing, but could switch to two feet for running
➡ herbivores

Ornithopods are divided into two sections in this book:

Early Ornithopods
➡ Were able to chew food
➡ Had sizable thumb spikes

Hadrosaurs
➡ Had elongated duckbills that helped them eat lots of plants
➡ Some had elaborate crests and horns on their heads

Some well-known ornithopods: *Iguanodon*, *Hadrosaurus*, *Parasaurolophus*

LATE JURASSIC

159 TO 144
MILLION YEARS AGO

Recognizable ornithopod features, such as duckbills and thumb spikes, evolved. Late Jurassic ornithopods browsed on four feet but remained bipedal when running from predators.

EARLY CRETACEOUS

144 TO 98
MILLION YEARS AGO

Many large hadrosaurs appeared; they had improved digestive systems that helped them thrive. Many ornithopods, including *Iguanodon*, had useful thumb spikes.

LATE CRETACEOUS

98 TO 66
MILLION YEARS AGO

Herds of large ornithopods browsed in Europe, Africa, and North America until all dinosaurs became extinct 66 million years ago.

DETAILS
63 EARLY ORNITHOPODS

BASAL ORNITHOPODS

Name	SIZE	AGE	FOSSILS	LOCATION
Albertadromeus (al-**BUR**-tah-droh-may-us)	S	LC	partial skeleton	NA
Atlascopcosaurus (at-las-**KOP**-koh-sore-us)	S	EC	teeth, bone	AU
Bugenasaura (boo-jen-uh-**SORE**-a)	M	LC	skull, bone	NA
Changchunsaurus (**CHANG**-choon-sore-us)	XS	EC	skull, bone	AS
Drinker (**DRIN**-kur)	S	LJ	partial skeleton	NA
Fulgurotherium (full-gur-oh-**THEE**-ree-um)	S	EC	partial skeleton	AU
Gasparinisaura (gas-pah-**REE**-nah-sore-a)	XS	LC	partial skeleton	SA
Haya (**HI**-yah)	S	LC	full skeleton	NA
Hypsilophodon (hip-shee-**LOH**-foe-don)	S	EC	full skeleton	EU
Jeholosaurus (jeh-**HOH**-loh-sore-us)	XS	EC	skull, partial skeleton, bone	AS
Koreanosaurus (core-**REE**-uh-no-sore-us)	UN	LC	partial skeleton	AS
Leaellynasaura (lee-el-in-a-**SORE**-a)	S	EC	teeth, skull, bone	AU
Notohypsilophodon (no-toe-hip-shee-**LOH**-foe-don)	S	LC	bone	SA
Orodromeus (or-oh-**DROH**-mee-us)	S	LC	bone	NA
Oryctodromeus (or-rik-toe-**DROH**-mee-us)	S	MC	partial skeleton	AS
Parkosaurus (**PAR**-koh-sore-us)	S	LC	skull, bone	NA
Qantassaurus (**KAN**-tas-sore-us)	S	EC	teeth	AU
Siluosaurus (**SY**-loh-sore-us)	UN	EC	teeth	AS
Thescelosaurus (**THESS**-keh-loh-sore-us)	M	MJ	partial skeleton	NA
Trinisaura (**TREE**-nee-sore-a)	XS	LC	partial skeleton	AN
Yandusaurus (**YAN**-doo-sore-us)	S	MJ	full skeleton	AS
Zephyrosaurus (**ZEH**-fih-roh-sore-us)	S	EC	skull, bone	NA

DRYOSAURS

Name	SIZE	AGE	FOSSILS	LOCATION
Anabisetia (**ANN**-uh-bee-seh-tee-uh)	S	LC	skull, bone	SA
Callovosaurus (cuh-**LOH**-voh-sore-us)	M	MJ	bone	EU
Dryosaurus (**DRY**-oh-sore-us)	M	MJ	partial skeleton, bone	NA/AF
Dysalotosaurus (dih-suh-**LOH**-toe-sore-us)	M	LJ	bone	AF
Elrhazosaurus (el-**RA**-zoh-sore-us)	XS	EC	bone	AF
Kangnasaurus (**KANG**-nuh-sore-us)	S	EC	teeth, skull	AF
Mochlodon (**MOK**-loh-don)	M	LC		EU
Muttaburrasaurus (moo-tuh-**BUR**-uh-sore-us)	L	EC	partial skeleton, bone	AU
Rhabdodon (**RAB**-doh-don)	M	LC	bone	EU

Name	SIZE	AGE	FOSSILS	LOCATION
Talenkauen (**TAH**-len-kon)	M	LC	partial skeleton	SA
Tenontosaurus (ten-**ON**-toh-sore-us)	L	EC	partial skeleton	NA
Valdosaurus (**VAL**-doh-sore-us)	S	EC	teeth, bone	EU
Zalmoxes (**ZAL**-mok-zees)	S	LC	skull	EU

IGUANODONTIDS

Name	SIZE	AGE	FOSSILS	LOCATION
Barilium (bah-**RIH**-lee-um)	L	LJ	partial skeleton	EU
Camptosaurus (**CAMP**-toe-sore-us)	L	EC	full skeleton	NA/EU
Cedrorestes (see-droh-**RES**-teez)	M	EC	partial skeleton	NA
Cumnoria (kum-**NOH**-ree-uh)	M	LJ	skull, bone	EU
Dakotadon (dah-koh-tuh-don)	M	EC	skull	NA
Darwinsaurus (**DAR**-win-sore-us)	M	EC	teeth, bone	EU
Delapparentia (**DAY**-lap-uh-ren-tee-uh)	L	EC	partial skeleton	EU
Dollodon (**DOLL**-oh-don)	M	EC	full skeleton	EU
Draconyx (drah-**KON**-iks)	L	LJ	bone	EU
Hippodraco (**HIP**-oh-dray-koh)	M	EC	skull, bone	NA
Huxleysaurus (**HUCKS**-lee-sore-us)	UN	EC	bone	EU
Hypselospinus (hip-sell-oh-**SPY**-nuss)	M	EC	teeth, bone	EU
Iguanacolossus (ih-**GWA**-no-koh-lah-suss)	L	EC	partial skeleton	NA
Iguanodon (ih-**GWA**-noh-don)	XL	EC	full skeleton, bone	EU/AF/NA
Kukufeldia (coo-coo-**FELL**-dee-uh)	L	EC	teeth, bone	EU
Lanzhousaurus (lan-joh-**SORE**-us)	XL	EC	skull	AS
Lurdusaurus (loor-duh-**SORE**-us)	L	EC	partial skeleton	AF
Mantellisaurus (man-**TEL**-ee-sore-us)	L	EC	skull, bone	EU
Mantellodon (man-**TEL**-oh-don)	L	EC		EU
Osmakasaurus (os-muh-kuh-**SORE**-us)	M	LC	partial skeleton	NA
Ouranosaurus (oo-**RAH**-noh-sore-us)	L	EC	partial skeleton	AF
Owenodon (oh-wen-oh-don)	UN	EC	bone	EU
Planicoxa (plan-ih-**KAHK**-suh)	L	EC	partial skeleton	NA
Proa (**PROH**-uh)	UN	EC	bone	EU
Proplanicoxa (proh-plan-ih-**KAHK**-suh)	M	EC	bone	EU
Sellacoxa (sel-uh-**KAHK**-suh)	L	EC	bone	EU
Theiophytalia (theeh-oh-fy-**TAY**-lee-a)	L	EC	skull	NA
Uteodon (yoot-**OH**-don)	M	LJ	full skeleton	NA

LEGEND

Featured dinosaurs are set in red in the list above.

SIZE
- XS — Under 5 feet
- S — 5-10 feet
- M — 10-20 feet
- L — 20-30 feet
- XL — 30-40 feet
- XXL — Over 40 feet
- UN — Unknown

AGE (years ago)
- LT — Late Triassic (227-201 million)
- EJ — Early Jurassic (201-180 million)
- MJ — Middle Jurassic (180-159 million)
- LJ — Late Jurassic (159-144 million)
- EC — Early Cretaceous (144-98 million)
- LC — Late Cretaceous (98-66 million)

FOSSILS
- Full skeleton
- Partial skeleton
- Skull
- Bone
- Teeth

LOCATION
- AS — Asia
- AF — Africa
- EU — Europe
- AU — Australia
- NA — North America
- SA — South America
- AN — Antarctica

O rnithopods, including *Iguanodon* and *Dryosaurus*, arrived fairly late in the Age of Dinosaurs; none have been found that lived before the Middle Jurassic period. They came with a set of practical advantages: teeth that could chew thoroughly; the ability to switch from walking on four feet to running on two feet; and big thumb spikes for foraging food and scaring away predators. This group showed how dinosaurs evolved traits that helped them survive.

Thescelosaurus

Rhabdodon

An ornithopod had a complicated set of teeth spaced throughout its mouth. These teeth—called a tooth battery—allowed it to chew its food thoroughly. This meant it could break down tough vegetation for easier digestion and to extract the most nutrients. Being able to stand on two legs and run fast to escape predators was another advantage.

HYPSILOPHODON

➡ A bipedal herbivore, thought to be a fast runner
➡ Name means "high-crested tooth" in Greek
➡ Was about 6 feet long; weighed about 100 pounds
➡ Had a triangular beak for snipping off low-growing vegetation, and cheek teeth that got sharper with use

FUN FACT *Hypsilophodon*'s name refers to the bony ridge on its head, not the teeth in its mouth.

CAMPTOSAURUS

➡ A bipedal herbivore with a sturdy body
➡ Named for its forward-leaning posture (*kamptos* means "flexible" in Greek)
➡ Was 20 feet long; weighed about 2,200 pounds
➡ Had a hornlike beak with more than 100 teeth

FUN FACT *Camptosaurus* could walk on two or four legs; it probably walked on all fours while browsing on low-growing vegetation.

DRYOSAURUS

➡ A bipedal herbivore with long, thin legs and short arms

➡ Named for its oak-leaf-shaped cheek teeth (*drys* means "oak" in Greek)

➡ Was up to 14 feet long; weighed about 180 pounds

➡ Had strong legs that gave it speed to escape predators

FUN FACT Juvenile and adult fossils have been found at Dinosaur National Monument, including the most complete juvenile *Dryosaurus* skull ever found.

OURANOSAURUS

➡ A bipedal herbivore that ate leaves, fruits, and seeds

➡ Named for the word for "brave" in Tuareg, a language of the area in Africa where it was discovered

➡ Was 20–25 feet long; weighed 5,000–8,000 pounds

➡ Had a long, flat head and a long snout

FUN FACT *Ouranosaurus* had a large, fan-shaped sail extending from its back; this may have been used to regulate body temperature in the hot desert climate in which it lived.

Large and bulky, *Iguanodon* had all the ornithopod advantages: It could switch from running on two legs to walking on four legs; it had cheek teeth that allowed it to chew its food thoroughly; and it had big, multipurpose thumb spikes. The front of its beak was toothless, but it had 29 big teeth in each cheek. Its beak was sharp enough to snip off vegetation, and its cheeks were spacious enough to hold food while the teeth ground it up. This made for easy digestion. *Iguanodon* also had a flexible pinkie finger to help it grasp and gather food. These eating aids helped keep it well fed and strong; it was one of the biggest ornithopods and, using its bulk and its thumb spikes, could survive fights with carnivores.

THUMBS UP!

Iguanodon's thumb spike had several possible uses. It was as long as 6 inches and very thick, making it a good weapon against carnivores that preyed upon *Iguanodon*. Some scientists think it was most useful for breaking up fruit and gathering food, like a built-in knife; some think the thumb spike made *Iguanodon* attractive to mates; and some think it was used to fight off rivals.

EUREKA!

Nearly two centuries ago, a doctor named Gideon Mantell found some large teeth in a forest near Sussex, England. At that time, around 1822, the only dinosaur bones and teeth that had been identified and named were those of *Megalosaurus*, a carnivore. Dr. Mantell believed that the big teeth he had found, along with some bones, belonged to a plant-eating dinosaur. He took them to some experts, who told him they were probably the teeth of a fish or a rhinoceros. Later, another expert accepted Dr. Mantell's findings, and *Iguanodon* became the first plant-eating dinosaur to be named.

PALEO DATA

IGUANODON

PRONUNCIATION
ih-**GWAN**-uh-don

SIZE
30 feet long; weighed
7,000–10,000 pounds

AGE
Early Cretaceous, about
130–110 million years ago

LOCATION
Europe, northern Africa,
western and northern
United States

FOSSILS
Many bones and skeletons

DIET
Plants

OOPS!

In 1878, some mine workers in Bernissart, Belgium, discovered a large buried *Iguanodon* skeleton. After digging further, paleontologists found 38 partial skeletons at the site. Following examination, it was determined that the fossils from the earlier find in England had been assembled incorrectly: A spike that actually belonged on *Iguanodon*'s thumb had been placed on its nose by mistake.

Length is the main measurement by which dinosaurs are compared. Dinosaur measurements are sometimes based on only a few bones or a single skeleton. It's difficult to know if that bone or skeleton is average for that type of dinosaur or the largest one ever, but scientists make assumptions based on the facts they have.

TEN LONGEST DINOSAURS

Dinosaur length is measured from the tip of the tail to the tip of the snout. This list is based on numbers officially recorded in scientific journals.

Argentinosaurus
98–118 feet

Mamenchisaurus: 50–115 feet

Supersaurus: 108–112 feet

Sauroposeidon: 92–112 feet

Futalongkosaurus: 92–112 feet

Diplodocus
98–108 feet

Antarctosaurus: 108 feet

Paralititan: 85–105 feet

Puertasaurus: 98 feet

Apatosaurus
70-90 feet

Epidexipteryx

SHORTEST DINOSAURS

Epidexipteryx:
9.8 inches

Parvicursor:
12 inches

Biggest or smallest, heaviest or lightest, dinosaurs came in all shapes and sizes.

LONGEST BY SUBORDER OR GROUP

LONGEST THEROPOD
Spinosaurus
47–59 feet

LONGEST SAUROPOD
Argentinosaurus
98–118 feet

LONGEST THYREOPHORAN
Stegosaurus
23–30 feet

LONGEST ORNITHOPOD
Huaxiaosaurus
61 feet

LONGEST MARGINOCEPHALIAN
Triceratops
30 feet

HOW DO YOU MEASURE THE LENGTH OF A DINOSAUR?

Paleontologists can estimate the total length of a dinosaur with only a few bones to work from. They do this by using complete skeletons of other dinosaurs to develop sets of relative measurements, based on the sizes of significant bones such as the femur, vertebrae, and skull. For example, if the femur in a complete *Brachiosaurus* skeleton is 14.2 percent of the total length of the animal, they infer that the femur of an *Argentinosaurus* is also 14.2 percent of its total length.

Extreme Dinosaurs

Records are made to be broken, especially in the world of dinosaurs. Often there's a clear winner; sometimes there's a tie. These dinosaurs may not stay in the top positions for long, as new discoveries take their places.

Sauroposeidon

TALLEST

(measured at the hip)

Sauroposeidon: 60 feet tall

Supersaurus: 40 feet tall

Brachiosaurus: 40 feet tall

SMARTEST

Intelligence estimates are based on the relationship between the size of the brain and the size of the body. Dinosaurs with high brain-to-body ratios are thought to have been more intelligent.

Troodon

Dromaeosaurus

Deinonychus

Deinonychus

Argentinosaurus

HEAVIEST

Argentinosaurus:
146,000 pounds

Puertasaurus:
146,000 pounds

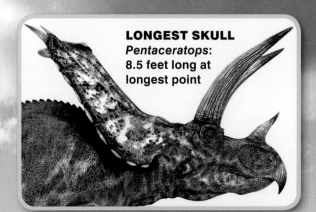

LONGEST SKULL
Pentaceratops:
8.5 feet long at
longest point

FASTEST

Speed estimates are based on the distances between footprints in fossilized dinosaur tracks. Scientists have developed computations that take into account the weight of the animal (based on how deep the tracks are) and the height of the animal. For example, if the animal was 10 feet high and weighed 1,000 pounds, and the tracks are two feet apart, the animal was running 15 miles per hour.

Gallimimus: 43 miles per hour

Ornithomimus: 43 miles per hour

Gallimimus

HOW DO YOU WEIGH A DINOSAUR?

Since there aren't any live dinosaurs around to put on a scale, their weights are estimates based on a combination of factors. Scientists include the weight of the bones and add an estimated amount for skin, muscle, and fat, based on the type of dinosaur. If tracks are found, experts can make an estimate based on how deep the tracks are, since heavier dinosaurs made deeper tracks.

IT'S ALL RELATIVE

DIPLODOCUS, one of the largest dinosaurs: 98–108 feet long; 16 feet tall; weighed 100,000–200,000 pounds

AFRICAN ELEPHANT, the largest living land animal: 11.5 feet tall; weighs 13,230 pounds

HUMAN (average size): 5.5 feet tall; weighs 150 pounds

DUCKBILLS

Name	SIZE	AGE	FOSSILS	LOCATION
Acristavus (ak-riss-**TAY**-vuss)	M	LC	Skull, Bone	NA
Altirhinus (al-tih-**RY**-nuss)	L	EC	Skull, Partial skeleton, Bone	AS
Anasazisaurus (ann-ah-sahz-ee-**SORE**-us)	XL	LC	Skull	NA
Bactrosaurus (**BAK**-troh-sore-us)	M	LC	Partial skeleton, Bone	AS
Barsboldia (**BARS**-boll-dee-yah)	L	LC	Bone	AS
Batyrosaurus (bah-**TY**-roe-sore-us)	M	LC	Partial skeleton	AS
Bolong (bo-long)	UN	EC	Skull, Bone	AS
Brachylophosaurus (**BRAK**-ee-loh-foh-sore-us)	M	LC	Bone	NA
Claosaurus (**CLAY**-oh-sore-us)	M	LC	Bone	NA
Edmontosaurus (ed-**MAHN**-toh-sore-us)	XXL	LC	Partial skeleton	NA
Eolambia (ee-oh-**LAM**-bee-uh)	L	LC	Partial skeleton	NA
Equijubus (ee-kwee-**JOO**-bus)	XL	EC	Skull	AS
Fukuisaurus (foo-**KOO**-ee-sore-us)	M	MC	Skull	AS
Gilmoreosaurus (**GILL**-mor-oh-sore-us)	L	LC	Partial skeleton	AS
Glishades (glih-**SHAYDS**)	UN	LC	Bone	NA
Gryposaurus (**GRIH**-poh-sore-us)	L	LC	Skull, Bone	NA
Hadrosaurus (hay-droh-**SORE**-us)	L	LC	Bone	NA
Huaxiaosaurus (**WOK**-see-ow-sore-us)	XXL	LC	Bone	AS
Huehuecanauhtlus (way-way-kan-**OUT**-luss)	UN	LC	Skull, Bone	NA
Jeyawati (hay-uh-**WAH**-tee)	M	MC/LC	Partial skeleton	NA
Jintasaurus (jin-tah-**SORE**-us)	UN	EC	Skull	AS
Jinzhousaurus (jin-show-oo-**SORE**-us)	L	EC	Partial skeleton	AS
Kerberosaurus (**CUR**-berr-oh-sore-us)	L	LC	Skull	EU
Kritosaurus (**CRY**-toe-sore-us)	L	LC	Skull, Bone	NA
Kundurosaurus (kun-door-roh-**SORE**-us)	UN	LC	Partial skeleton	AS
Latirhinus (la-tih-**RY**-nuss)	L	LC	Partial skeleton	NA
Levnesovia (lev-nuh-**SOH**-vee-a)	L	LC	Skull, Bone	AS
Lophorhothon (loh-for-**HOH**-thon)	M	LC	Skull, Bone	NA
Maiasaura (my-ya-**SORE**-a)	XL	LC	Partial skeleton	NA
Naashoibitosaurus (nah-ah-shoh-ee-**BEE**-toe-sore-us)	L	LC	Skull, Partial skeleton	NA
Nanyangosaurus (**NAN**-ee-ang-oh-sore-us)	M	EC	Partial skeleton, Bone	AS
Penelopognathus (**PEN**-uh-loh-poh-nay-thus)	M	EC	Bone	AS
Probactrosaurus (proh-bak-troh-**SORE**-us)	M	MC	Partial skeleton, Bone	AS
Prosaurolophus (proh-soh-**ROH**-loh-fuss)	L	LC	Skull, Partial skeleton, Bone	NA
Protohadros (**PROH**-toe-ha-dros)	M	LC	Skull, Bone	NA
Saurolophus (**SORE**-oh-loh-fuss)	XL	LC	Partial skeleton, Bone	NA/AS
Secernosaurus (see-sur-no-**SORE**-us)	S	LC	Skull, Bone	SA
Shantungosaurus (shahn-**DUNG**-oh-sore-us)	XXL	LC	Partial skeleton, Bone	AS
Shuangmiaosaurus (shoo-ang-**ME**-ow-sore-us)	L	MC	Bone	AS
Tanius (**TAN**-ee-us)	L	LC	Teeth, Bone	AS
Telmatosaurus (tell-**MA**-toh-sore-us)	M	LC	Bone	EU
Tethyshadros (**TEH**-thiss-hay-dross)	M	LC	Bone	EU
Willinakaqe (weel-yee-nah-**KAH**-gay)	L	LC	Bone	AS
Wulagasaurus (woo-**LAH**-guh-SORE-us)	XL	LC	Bone	AS
Xuwulong (zhoo-woo-**LONG**)	UN	EC	Skull, Partial skeleton, Bone	AS
Zhanghenglong (jhang-heng-long)	UN	LC	Skull	AS

CRESTED DUCKBILLS

Name	SIZE	AGE	FOSSILS	LOCATION
Amurosaurus (a-mur-oh-**SORE**-us)	M	LC	Bone	EU/AS
Angulomastacator (ann-goo-low-**MASS**-tah-kah-tore)	L	LC	Bone	NA
Aralosaurus (**AR**-uh-lo-sore-us)	L	LC	Partial skeleton, Bone	AS
Arenysaurus (**AR**-ehn-ee-sore-us)	M	LC	Skull, Partial skeleton, Bone	EU
Blasisaurus (**BLAYZ**-ee-sore-us)	UN	LC	Partial skeleton, Bone	EU
Canardia (can-ahr-dee-uh)	UN	LC	Bone	EU
Charonosaurus (char-**ON**-oh-sore-us)	XXL	LC	Skull	AS
Corythosaurus (co-**RIH**-thoh-sore-us)	L	LC	Skull	NA
Hypacrosaurus (hi-**PA**-krow-SORE-us)	L	LC	Skull	NA
Jaxartosaurus (jak-**SAR**-toe-SORE-us)	L	LC	Skull	AS
Kazaklambia (kah-zahk-lam-**BEE**-uh)	UN	LC	Bone	AS
Lambeosaurus (**LAM**-bee-oh-SORE-us)	XL	LC	Partial skeleton, Bone	NA
Magnapaulia (mag-nuh-**PAW**-lee-uh)	XXL	LC	Skull, Partial skeleton, Bone	NA
Nanningosaurus (**NAH**-ning-oh-sore-us)	UN	LC	Partial skeleton, Bone	AS
Nipponosaurus (nee-**PAH**-noh-sore-us)	L	LC	Skull, Partial skeleton, Bone	AS
Olorotitan (oh-loh-**roh**-titan)	L	LC	Partial skeleton, Bone	EU
Pararhabdodon (**PAR**-a-rab-do-don)	M	LC	Skull, Bone	EU
Parasaurolophus (**PAR**-ah-sore-ah-loh-fuss)	XL	LC	Skull, Partial skeleton, Bone	NA
Sahaliyania (suh-ha-lee-**AH**-nee-uh)	XL	LC	Skull	AS
Tsintaosaurus (sin-tauw-**SORE**-us)	XL	LC	Partial skeleton, Bone	AS
Velafrons (**VEL**-uh-frons)	XL	LC	Skull, Partial skeleton, Bone	NA

LEGEND

Featured dinosaurs are set in red in the list above.

SIZE
- XS — Under 5 feet
- S — 5-10 feet
- M — 10-20 feet
- L — 20-30 feet
- XL — 30-40 feet
- XXL — Over 40 feet
- UN — Unknown

AGE (years ago)
- LT — Late Triassic (227-201 million)
- EJ — Early Jurassic (201-180 million)
- MJ — Middle Jurassic (180-159 million)
- LJ — Late Jurassic (159-144 million)
- EC — Early Cretaceous (144-98 million)
- LC — Late Cretaceous (98-66 million)

FOSSILS
- Full skeleton
- Partial skeleton
- Skull
- Bone
- Teeth

LOCATION
- AS — Asia
- AF — Africa
- EU — Europe
- AU — Australia
- NA — North America
- SA — South America
- AN — Antarctica

Hadrosaurs Ornithopods

Hadrosaurs (*hadro* means "big") lived in the forests of Europe, Asia, and North America in the Late Cretaceous period. Their common name is duckbill, because the heads of some members resembled those of modern ducks. They had long, flat bills or short beaks that were just right for snipping twigs and leaves from trees. Some, including *Corythosaurus*, had crests on their heads.

Brachylophosaurus

Hadrosaur Headgear

Hadrosaurs were big, sturdy dinosaurs with a very practical set of teeth and a useful ability to switch from walking on four feet to running on two feet. Many of them had flat bills to snip off plant leaves efficiently. They also sported headgear that seemed to be for display purposes only. But experts theorize that the horns, spikes, and crests on their heads may have been used to attract mates or make their vocalizations—sounds—louder.

LAMBEOSAURUS

➡ A bipedal herbivore that ate pine needles, leaves, and twigs

➡ Named for an early Canadian paleontologist, Lawrence Lambe

➡ Was 30–50 feet long; weighed 8,000–12,000 pounds

➡ Had a large, hollow crest on its head that may have been used to produce sounds

FUN FACT *Lambeosaurus* was the largest of the duckbills.

DID YOU KNOW?

Maiasaura's name is the feminine form—*saura* instead of *saurus*—because the dinosaur is so closely connected to mothering.

MAIASAURA

➡ A quadrupedal herbivore that lived in herds; fossils of about 10,000 were discovered together in Montana

➡ Name means "good mother lizard" (Maia was a mother in Greek mythology)— it was the first dinosaur found near its nest, eggs, and hatchlings

➡ Was about 30 feet long; weighed 6,000 pounds

➡ Stayed near its nest, but was too heavy to brood (sit on) its eggs

FUN FACT *Maiasaura* was the first dinosaur in space—small pieces of *Maiasaura* bone and eggshell were carried by physicist Loren Acton on NASA's Spacelab-2 mission in 1985.

EDMONTOSAURUS

- ➡ A bipedal herbivore that stood on all fours to eat low-growing vegetation
- ➡ Named for the Edmonton rock formation in Alberta, Canada, where it was first discovered
- ➡ Was 40 feet long; weighed 6,000 pounds
- ➡ Had hundreds of teeth, and muscular cheek pouches to grind up its food

FUN FACT *Edmontosaurus* may have lived in herds; fossils of several animals have been discovered together.

DR. JOE SAYS

Fossils of *Edmontosaurus* with skin impressions have been found, from Canada to Montana to South Dakota. These fossils, often called dinosaur "mummies," give paleontologists a rare window into what dinosaur skin looked like. Skin impressions from the head of *Edmontosaurus* show that it had a soft crest, like a chicken's.
— *Dr. Joseph Sertich, Paleontologist*

PARASAUROLOPHUS

- ➡ A bipedal herbivore; fossilized stomach contents included plants
- ➡ Named for the long, backward-facing crest on its head (*para* means "beside" and *lophos* means "crest" in Greek)
- ➡ Was 33 feet long; weighed about 4,000 pounds
- ➡ Had nostrils that formed tubes up to the crest, which may have been used to make sounds

FUN FACT Experts initially thought *Parasaurolophus* lived in the water and used its crest as a snorkel, but based on additional study and evidence, they now think it lived on land.

Working With Dinosaurs

Paleontologists may work in museums, universities, or science laboratories. Some paleontologists go on digs to find new bones and species and then bring fossils back for further study.

WHAT DO PALEONTOLOGISTS DO?

➡ Paleontologists look for and study dinosaur bones.

➡ They go on digs and use precision tools such as pickaxes, shovels, brushes, and chisels to remove dirt from bones without harming them. They take photographs and record their findings.

➡ When they find fossils, paleontologists carefully unearth and pack them. The fossils are sent to laboratories for study and testing.

➡ Fossils are analyzed and reassembled into skeletons.

➡ Findings are written about and published in science journals so the world can share in the discovery.

DR. JOE SAYS

My favorite part of paleontology is the thrill of discovery. Often, we work in very difficult conditions in very hot, cold, windy, or rainy weather and spend many weeks or months away from home camping in remote areas. It is all worth it, though, when we discover a new dinosaur or a spectacular fossil!

— *Dr. Joseph Sertich, Paleontologist*

DINO DETECTIVE

SHIPPING

When fossils need to be shipped—from the discovery site to a lab or from a lab to a museum where they will be displayed—paleontologists pack bones carefully. They wrap them in soft materials and sometime set them in plaster of paris—like a cast on a broken leg—so that they arrive at a lab intact. Sometimes, the wrapped bones are airlifted from the discovery site, by plane or helicopter. Before shipping, every crate or package is sealed, labeled, and recorded.

People who love dinosaurs and want to spend their lives studying them become paleontologists or choose another career that involves the prehistoric world.

GETTING STARTED:
A CAREER IN PALEONTOLOGY

→ **LEARN TO OBSERVE** Paleontologists find bones by noticing subtle shifts in rocks and soil. Start now by observing everything around you.

→ **TAKE NOTES AND KEEP RECORDS** Write down what you see; practice taking good notes.

→ **STUDY STEM SUBJECTS** STEM = Science, Technology, Engineering, and Math. Life science, Earth science, and math, in particular, will help you understand the dinosaurs' world and how to assess it.

→ **PRACTICE WRITING** Paleontologists spend much of their time writing books and papers about dinosaurs and other prehistoric life.

→ **GO ON DIGS** Find a museum or school program that organizes digs in your area. If you can't find one, talk to a science teacher and see if you can set one up.

→ **WORK HARD FOR GOOD GRADES** Most paleontologists have advanced degrees, including doctorates. Be prepared for a long education.

→ **STAY IN SHAPE** Paleontologists have to be physically fit to endure hard work in tight spaces, sometimes in cold or hot climates.

Bone Hunters

From the earliest days of dinosaur discoveries, bone hunters devoted their lives to advancing our knowledge of these prehistoric creatures. They organized digs all over the world to find new species. In the early part of the last century, only three dinosaurs were known; by its end, there were hundreds.

THREE FAMOUS DINOSAUR HUNTERS

Megalosaurus

Allosaurus

Coelophysis

SIR RICHARD OWEN (1804–1892)

A British scientist, Sir Richard Owen spent most of his time studying the anatomy of living things. By the 1830s, he became interested in fossils of extinct animals. He studied the fossils of three large species: the carnivore *Megalosaurus*, and herbivores *Iguanodon* and *Hylaeosaurus*. It was Owen who first stated that these animals were part of an unknown group of prehistoric creatures. He established a scientific order for them and named it "Dinosauria."

OTHNIEL CHARLES (O. C.) MARSH (1831–1899)

Born in Connecticut, O. C. Marsh traveled throughout the world when he was a young man, studying all kinds of animals and rocks. When he returned to America, he convinced his wealthy uncle, George Peabody, to establish the Peabody Museum at Yale University. Marsh discovered 100 new dinosaur species, including *Apatosaurus* and *Allosaurus*. He also named the theropod, sauropod, and ornithopod suborders.

EDWARD DRINKER COPE (1840–1897)

An American paleontologist who led many expeditions to the American West in search of new dinosaurs, Edward Drinker Cope discovered, described, and named 56 dinosaurs. He traveled throughout Europe and the United States and worked himself and his colleagues mercilessly as he strove for more and better information. He was also a specialist in fish and snakes. Cope wrote more than 1,400 scientific articles about animals. The dinosaur *Drinker* is named for him.

For centuries people found huge bones while farming, mining, and during construction. But no one knew what they were until the 1850s, when scientists realized that they belonged to a group of extraordinary animals, and dinosaurs were given a name.

THE BONE WARS

O. C. Marsh and Edward Drinker Cope met in Berlin and soon became bitter rivals. Each was determined to outdo the other in finding and naming new dinosaurs. When one of them published an article about a discovery, the other would write that it was not significant. In the end, Cope named 56 dinosaurs and Marsh named 100; both contributed immensely to our knowledge of the Age of Dinosaurs.

KEEPING RECORDS

One of the most important tasks that a paleontologist has to do when finding a fossil is take detailed notes. A paleontologist will write down exactly where and when the find was made and what else was in the area. Rock samples and many photographs are taken. All the information is recorded in notebooks and computer documents.

OOPS! MAJOR MISTAKES AND MISHAPS

Even the most expert paleontologists sometimes made mistakes—and often published information that was later proven false.

➜ Sir Richard Owen had a model created of *Megalosaurus*, the first dinosaur ever named. But it was later discovered that many of the bones used in the model came from other dinosaurs.

➜ Edward Drinker Cope discovered the fossils of *Amphicoelias*, possibly the longest dinosaur ever discovered; he estimated its size at about 190 feet. But the bones disappeared (they may have disintegrated because ways of preserving fossils had not yet been invented), and the find can't be authenticated.

➜ O. C. Marsh theorized that *Stegosaurus* had a second brain in its hip or rump because he could not believe such a big animal could survive with such a small brain. His theory has since been proven false.

The field of paleontology has come a long way since the first bone hunters made the first discoveries and had some mix-ups along the way. Today, modern equipment and a vast body of knowledge make it easier to understand dinosaurs. But there is still much to be learned, and the next generation of paleontologists will learn even more about how dinosaurs lived and how their bodies worked.

WORKING PALEONTOLOGISTS

DR. LINDSAY ZANNO

(Director, Paleontology & Geology Research Laboratory, North Carolina Museum of Natural Sciences)
Dr. Zanno studies theropod dinosaurs and their varied diets. She is an expert on raptors and on therizinosaurs, plant-eating theropods with terrifyingly long claws.

DR. PHILIP J. CURRIE

(Professor, University of Alberta)
Dr. Currie is one of the leading paleontologists of our time. In the 1980s, his expeditions to China led to pioneering research into feathered dinosaurs. He is also an expert on the origin of birds and on migration and herding patterns. Dr. Currie helped found the Royal Tyrrell Museum in Alberta and created models that showed how *Diplodocus* whipped its tail.

DR. SCOTT D. SAMPSON

(Vice President of Research and Collections, Denver Museum of Nature & Science)
Dr. Sampson is a dinosaur paleontologist, evolutionary biologist, and science communicator. He studies the ecology and evolution of Late Cretaceous dinosaurs. His projects include books (*Dinosaur Odyssey: Fossil Threads in the Web of Life*) and TV shows (*Dinosaur Train, Dinosaur Planet*).

DR. RANDALL IRMIS

(Curator of Paleontology, Natural History Museum of Utah)
Dr. Irmis is an expert on very early dinosaurs and how they evolved from archosaurs. He studies how dinosaurs adapted to climate change over long time spans and why remains become fossilized. He uses high-tech tools to date the rocks containing the fossils.

RECENT DISCOVERIES

In 1990, paleontologist Sue Hendrickson discovered the most complete *T. rex* ever found. Studying this skeleton yielded tremendous information about dinosaurs.

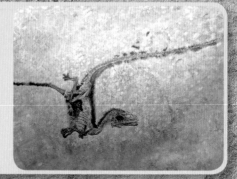

In 1996, researchers in China named *Sinosauropteryx*, one of the first birdlike dinosaurs to leave impressions of feathers. Since then, many other feathered dinosaurs have been found.

In 1975, Jack Horner was visiting a fossil shop in South Dakota when he found nests, eggs, and embryos of *Maiasaura*. Our knowledge of dinosaur nesting and hatching started then.

NEW SCIENCE

New tools make paleontologists' work easier and more effective.

Electron microscopes can magnify bones to hundreds of thousands of times their original size; scientists can see features as small as pigment molecules in fossilized feathers.

Satellite images help us find hidden outcrops of rocks that may hold not-yet-discovered dinosaurs.

CT scans, MRIs, and X-rays can find tiny structures and nerve pathways in brain cases or other anatomical structures. From these pictures, scientists can learn about how dinosaur bodies worked.

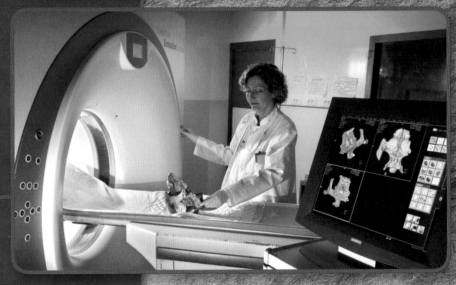

Images of dinosaur bones can be created on 3D imaging computers.

Computers allow huge amounts of information to be stored, sorted, and classified.

Protoceratops

These dinosaurs are known for their heads—their other features pale in comparison. Members of the largest group, known as ceratopsians ("horn faces"), had huge skulls with elaborate arrangements of pointy horns on them; some also had frills. Members of a second, smaller group, known as thick-headed dinosaurs, had small caps or domes of bone covering their skulls.

All marginocephalians were herbivores and mostly quadrupedal. They had large beaks and jaws filled with teeth. Stout and slow moving, they kept their heads down as they browsed and may have used their heads to defend themselves from the carnivores that shared their habitats.

LATE TRIASSIC	EARLY JURASSIC	MIDDLE JURASSIC
227 TO 201 MILLION YEARS AGO	**201 TO 180** MILLION YEARS AGO	**180 TO 159** MILLION YEARS AGO
No marginocephalian fossils have been found from this period yet.	No marginocephalian fossils have been found from this period yet.	No marginocephalian fossils have been found from this period yet.

Horns and Fringes
Marginocephalians

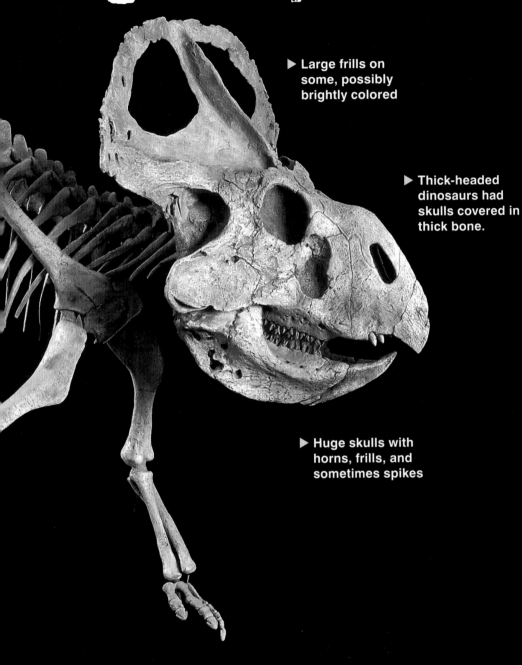

▶ Large frills on some, possibly brightly colored

▶ Thick-headed dinosaurs had skulls covered in thick bone.

▶ Huge skulls with horns, frills, and sometimes spikes

AT A GLANCE

The word *marginocephalian* means "fringe head." Members of this group had attachments on their heads. One group, ceratopsians, had horns, spikes, and frills; a second group, thick-headed dinosaurs, had domes of bony material covering their skulls. Marginocephalian fossils have been found in Europe, Asia, and North America. There are 85 known marginocephalians.

Marginocephalians were:
➜ part of the ornithischian (bird-hipped) order of dinosaurs
➜ quadrupedal
➜ herbivores

Marginocephalians are divided into two sections in this book:

Ceratopsians
➜ Had complicated and useful beaks and teeth
➜ Were known for elaborate horns and frills on their skulls

Thick-Headed Dinosaurs
➜ Had rounded, bony domes on their heads
➜ Probably used their thick skulls to butt the flanks of competitors

Some well-known marginocephalians: *Stegoceras*, *Triceratops*, *Pachycephalosaurus*

LATE JURASSIC

159 TO 144
MILLION YEARS AGO

Yinlong, the earliest known ceratopsian, was from this period; it's the only one that lived prior to the Cretaceous period that has been discovered.

EARLY CRETACEOUS

144 TO 98
MILLION YEARS AGO

During this period, a few more early ceratopsians, including *Psittacosaurus*, appeared.

LATE CRETACEOUS

98 TO 66
MILLION YEARS AGO

Marginocephalians, including *Triceratops*, became common in the latter part of this period, toward the end of the Age of Dinosaurs.

DINO DETAILS
68 CERATOPSIANS MARGINOCEPHALIANS

FIRST HORNED FACES

Name	SIZE	AGE	FOSSILS	LOCATION
Ajkaceratops (eye-kah-**SERR**-a-tops)	XS	LC	Skull	EU
Albalophosaurus (al-bah-**LOH**-foe-sore-us)	UN	EC	Skull	AS
Archaeoceratops (ahr-kee-oh-**SERR**-a-tops)	XS	EC	Partial skeleton	AS
Asiaceratops (ay-zha-**SERR**-a-tops)	S	LC	Bone	AS
Auroraceratops (aw-roh-rah-**SERR**-a-tops)	XS	EC		AS
Bagaceratops (bag-uh-**SERR**-a-tops)	XS	LC		AS
Bainoceratops (bain-oh-**SERR**-a-tops)	S	LC	Bone	AS
Cerasinops (**SERR**-uh-sin-ops)	S	LC	Partial skeleton	NA
Chaoyangsaurus (chow-yahng-**SORE**-us)	S	EC		AS
Gobiceratops (go-bee-**SERR**-a-tops)	XS	LC	Skull	AS
Graciliceratops (gras-ill-ih-**SERR**-a-tops)	XS	EC	Partial skeleton	AS
Gryphoceratops (griff-oh-**SERR**-a-tops)	XS	LC		NA
Helioceratops (hee-lee-oh-**SERR**-a-tops)	XS	EC	Bone	AS
Hongshanosaurus (hong-**SHAN**-oh-sore-us)	S	EC	Skull	AS
Koreaceratops (core-ee-uh-**SERR**-a-tops)	S	EC		AS
Kulceratops (kool-**SERR**-a-tops)	UN	EC		AS
Lamaceratops (lam-ah-**SERR**-a-tops)	S	LC	Skull	AS
Leptoceratops (lep-toe-**SERR**-a-tops)	S	LC	Skull, Partial skeleton	AS
Liaoceratops (lee-ow-**SERR**-a-tops)	XS	EC	Full skeleton	NA
Magnirostris (mag-nih-**ROSS**-tris)	XS	LC	Skull	AS
Microceratus (my-croh-**SERR**-a-tuss)	XS	LC	Partial skeleton	AS
Micropachycephalosaurus (my-croh-pak-ee-seff-uh-loh-**SORE**-us)	XS	LC	Partial skeleton	AS
Montanoceratops (mon-tan-oh-**SERR**-a-tops)	S	LC	Partial skeleton	NA
Prenoceratops (preh-no-**SERR**-a-tops)	S	LC		NA
Protoceratops (proh-toh-**SERR**-a-tops)	S	LC	Bone	AS
Psittacosaurus (sit-ah-koh-**SORE**-us)	S	EC	Full skeleton	AS
Stenopelix (steh-**NAH**-pee-liks)	XS	EC	Partial skeleton	EU
Udanoceratops (oo-dahn-o-**SERR**-a-tops)	S	LC	Skull	AS
Unescoceratops (yoo-ness-coe-**SERR**-a-tops)	S	LC	Bone	NA
Xuanhuaceratops (shwan-hwa-**SERR**-a-tops)	XS	LC	Bone	AS
Yamaceratops (yah-muh-**SERR**-a-tops)	XS	EC	Skull, Partial skeleton	AS
Yinlong (yin-**LONG**)	XS	LJ	Full skeleton	AS
Zhuchengceratops (joo-cheng-**SERR**-a-tops)	S	LC	Teeth, Skull, Partial skeleton	AS

HORNED FACES

Name	SIZE	AGE	FOSSILS	LOCATION
Achelousaurus (ah-key-loh-uh-**SORE**-us)	M	LC	Partial skeleton	NA
Agathaumas (ah-gah-**THAU**-muss)	L	LC	Bone	NA
Agujaceratops (ah-goo-yah-**SERR**-a-tops)	M	LC	Partial skeleton	NA
Albertaceratops (al-burt-uh-**SERR**-a-tops)	M	LC	Skull	NA
Anchiceratops (an-key-**SERR**-a-tops)	M	LC	Skull	NA
Arrhinoceratops (A-ry-no-**SERR**-a-tops)	M	LC	Skull	NA
Avaceratops (ay-vuh-SERR-a-tops)	M	LC	Skull	NA
Brachyceratops (brak-ee-**SERR**-a-tops)	S	LC	Partial skeleton	NA
Centrosaurus (sen-tro-**SORE**-us)	M	LC	Skull	NA
Chasmosaurus (kas-mo-**SORE**-us)	L	LC	Partial skeleton	NA
Coahuilaceratops (co-ah-hwee-lah-**SERR**-a-tops)	L	LC	Skull, Partial skeleton	NA
Coronosaurus (core-oh-no-**SORE**-us)	M	LC	Skull	NA
Diabloceratops (dee-ah-bloh-**SERR**-a-tops)	L	LC	Skull	NA
Einiosaurus (eye-nee-oh-**SORE**-us)	M	LC	Skull	NA
Judiceratops (joo-dee-**SERR**-a-tops)	UN	LC	Skull	NA
Kosmoceratops (**KAHZ**-moh-**SERR**-a-tops)	M	LC	Skull	NA
Medusaceratops (meh-doo-sah-**SERR**-a-tops)	M	LC	Skull	NA
Mercuriceratops (muhr-cure-uh-**SERR**-a-tops)	UN	LC	Bone	NA
Mojoceratops (moh-joh-**SERR**-a-tops)	M	LC	Skull	NA
Monoclonius (mah-no-**CLOH**-nee-us)	M	LC	Skull, Partial skeleton	NA
Nasutoceratops (nah-soo-toe-**SERR**-a-tops)	M	LC	Skull, Partial skeleton	NA
Pachyrhinosaurus (pak-ee-ry-no-**SORE**-us)	M	LC	Skull	NA
Pentaceratops (pen-ta-**SERR**-a-tops)	L	LC	Skull, Partial skeleton	NA
Rubeosaurus (**ROO**-bee-oh-sore-us)	M	LC	Skull	NA
Sinoceratops (sy-no-**SERR**-a-tops)	M	LC	Skull	AS
Spinops (**SPY**-nops)	M	LC	Skull, Partial skeleton	NA
Styracosaurus (sty-**RAK**-oh-sore-us)	M	LC	Partial skeleton	NA
Tatankaceratops (tah-tank-uh-**SERR**-a-tops)	UN	LC	Skull	NA
Torosaurus (**TORE**-oh-sore-us)	L	LC	Skull, Partial skeleton	NA
Triceratops (try-**SERR**-a-tops)	L	LC	Partial skeleton	NA
Turanoceratops (too-rahn-oh-**SERR**-a-tops)	L	LC	Teeth, Skull, Partial skeleton	AS
Utahceratops (yoo-tah-**SERR**-a-tops)	M	LC	Skull	NA
Vagaceratops (vay-guh-**SERR**-a-tops)	M	LC	Skull	NA
Xenoceratops (zee-no-**SERR**-a-tops)	M	LC	Skull	NA
Zuniceratops (zoo-nee-**SERR**-a-tops)	M	MC	Skull, Partial skeleton	NA

LEGEND

Featured dinosaurs are set in red in the list above.

SIZE
- XS Under 5 feet
- S 5-10 feet
- M 10-20 feet
- L 20-30 feet
- XL 30-40 feet
- XXL Over 40 feet
- UN Unknown

AGE (years ago)
- LT Late Triassic (227-201 million)
- EJ Early Jurassic (201-180 million)
- MJ Middle Jurassic (180-159 million)
- LJ Late Jurassic (159-144 million)
- EC Early Cretaceous (144-98 million)
- LC Late Cretaceous (98-66 million)

FOSSILS
- Full skeleton
- Partial skeleton
- Skull
- Bone
- Teeth

LOCATION
- AS Asia
- AF Africa
- EU Europe
- AU Australia
- NA North America
- SA South America
- AN Antarctica

Ceratopsians
Marginocephalians

They weren't known for speed, size, or intelligence, but ceratopsian dinosaurs were certainly strange. Also called horned faces (*cera* means "horn"), *Triceratops* and its relatives had pointy horns all over their heads. Some also had sharp spikes sticking out in random places. To top it off, large frills grew out of their skulls. Some of these ceratopsian features had practical purposes and some were just for display. All of these dinosaurs were quadrupedal herbivores.

Torosaurus

Making a Point

s easy to recognize most of these dinosaurs by their horns, but they had
her important features as well. They had strong bodies, many teeth arranged
ectly for browsing, and hard beaks that may have been covered in a hard
ective coating called keratin, which is also found in human skin, hair, and nails.

STYRACOSAURUS

➡ A quadrupedal herbivore with short legs; experts think it may have run at up to 20 miles per hour

➡ Name means "spiked lizard" (*styrax* means "spike" in Greek)

➡ Was 18 feet long; weighed up to 6,000 pounds

➡ Was a many-horned dinosaur, with four to six horns on its neck frill, one on each cheek, and one on its beak, in addition to other frills and ridges on its skull

FUN FACT Bone beds (places where concentrations of fossils are found) show that many *Styracosaurus* died together, suggesting that they traveled in herds.

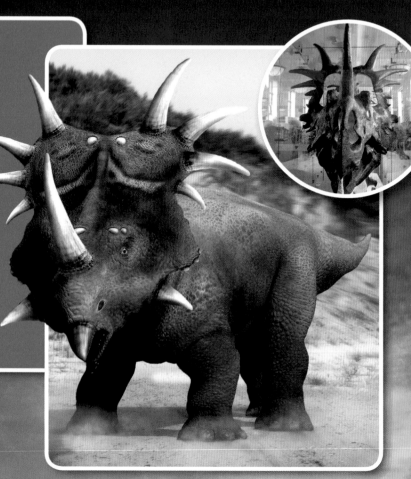

RATOPSIAN TOPPERS

Aquiaceratops

Centrosaurus

Zuniceratops

PROTOCERATOPS

➡ A quadrupedal herbivore that lived toward the end of the Age of Dinosaurs

➡ Name means "first horn-face" in Greek—but it wasn't the first ceratopsian

➡ Was 6 feet long; weighed about 400 pounds

➡ Had a large neck frill protruding from its skull

FUN FACT *Protoceratops* was prey for *Velociraptor* and *Tsaagan*, but herd living provided some safety in numbers.

PSITTACOSAURUS

➡ A bipedal herbivore; 11 different species have been identified, more than for any other dinosaur

➡ Named for its head, which was shaped like a parrot's (*psittakos* means "parrot" in Greek)

➡ Was about 4 feet long; weighed up to 40 pounds

➡ Had teeth and a beak that could chop off vegetation, but couldn't grind or chew; swallowed stones—called gastroliths—to grind up food during digestion

FUN FACT More than 400 individual *Psittacosaurus* fossils have been found, ranging in age from newborn to adult, making it a well-studied dinosaur.

Triceratops was one of the late arrivals on the dinosaur scene: It didn't appear until 69 million years ago, about 3 million years before all dinosaurs became extinct. It lived around the same time as *Tyrannosaurus rex*; skeletons of each have been found with scars from the teeth or horns of the other. *Triceratops* was a big, heavy animal with a huge skull—its head was about one-third the length of its whole body. Topping off its skull was an enormous frill, which pointed backward and extended as much as 7 feet. Along with its three horns (*tri* means "three" in Greek), this frill makes *Triceratops* one of the best-known dinosaurs.

DID YOU KNOW?

Many marginocephalians traveled in herds, but there is little evidence that *Triceratops* did. The largest groups found together included only three dinosaurs—in one case it was three juveniles, in another it was an adult and two juveniles. This indicates families rather than herds.

PALEO DATA

TRICERATOPS

PRONUNCIATION
tri-*SERR*-uh-tops

SIZE
25 feet long; weighed about 20,000 pounds

AGE
Late Cretaceous, about 69–66 million years ago

LOCATION
Western Canada and United States

FOSSILS
Many skulls, many partial skeletons, several complete skeletons

DIET
Plants

FOSSIL FILE

More than 50 *Triceratops* fossils were found in the Hell Creek Formation, an area that includes parts of Montana, North and South Dakota, and Wyoming, from 2000 to 2010—so many that one paleontologist, John Scannella, said that it was hard not to stumble upon one.

Different kinds of ceratopsians had different arrangements of horns, frills, and spikes when they were adults, but they looked alike when they were young. Their horns changed shape and size as they grew older; some of the horns vanished and others grew in.

What Killed the Dinosaurs?

Until 66 million years ago, a healthy population of dinosaurs inhabited Earth. Big carnivores such as *T. rex* were the dominant species. New species, including *Triceratops*, had popped up. And then, the fossil record shows, they all vanished. There is great debate about what happened, but scientists agree that a cataclysmic event occurred.

The dying off of dinosaurs and many other species 66 million years ago is called the K–T extinction. It marked the end of the Cretaceous (K) period and the beginning of the Tertiary (T) period. Not only dinosaurs died; more than 75 percent of all animal species did not survive the K–T extinction event and its aftermath. Scientists have many opinions about what happened, but there are two main theories—that a sudden, huge catastrophe occurred, wiping out most of animal life in a very short time; or that a series of disasters, including a significant change in climate, occurred over a longer period of time.

SLOWER: MANY VOLCANOES AND CHANGING CLIMATE

There is evidence that volcanoes were active around the time of the K–T extinction. If volcanic activity was heavy throughout the world, smoke, ash, and gas would have blocked out the sun and cooled the climate. As a result, much of the food supply for herbivores would have been destroyed. When the herbivores died off from starvation, carnivores would have lost their food supply and died off as well.

At the end of the Age of Dinosaurs, something big happened. What it was is a source of fascination for humankind—and a major area of study for experts.

FASTER: ONE BIG ASTEROID

What happened? The most widely-accepted theory is that a huge asteroid from space hit Earth, setting off tsunamis—massive tidal waves—and dust clouds all over the world. The reason scientists think this is because of the presence of a mineral called iridium in the layer of soil that dates back to the extinction time. Iridium is rare on Earth, but it is plentiful in asteroids. A truly massive asteroid would have been able to cause the damage that occurred in the K–T extinction in a matter of hours or days.

Protecting What Remains

There is nothing we can do to help the dinosaurs that died 66 million years ago. But we can make sure that the fossil record they left behind does not disappear as well.

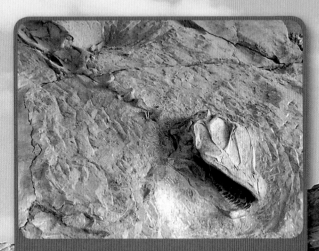

Fossils of many large dinosaurs, including *Cammarasaurus*, have been unearthed and can be viewed at Dinosaur National Monument on the Colorado-Utah border. And the Morrison Formation, which covers parts of Wyoming, Colorado, and other western states, is one of the most dinosaur-rich areas in the world.

PRESERVING FOSSILS

Human activities such as mining and construction can uncover incredible fossils—but they can also destroy fossils without anyone noticing. There are areas rich with fossils—particularly the western United States and Canada and parts of China and Argentina—that need protection, and paleontologists are working to ensure these areas remain intact for future discoveries. In addition, governments work to preserve fossil-rich land by creating national parks such as Florissant Fossil Beds National Monument and Dinosaur National Monument, and smaller state and private preserves (including Dinosaur State Park in Connecticut).

DID YOU KNOW?

Scientists estimate that more than 99 percent of species that have ever lived on Earth are now extinct.

Dinosaur National Monument includes more than 200,000 acres of mountains and canyons that are rich in fossils—thousands have been found here.

EXTINCTION IS FOREVER

While we don't know for sure what caused dinosaurs to die off, we do have some ideas as to why some animals alive today are threatened species. Pollution, high energy usage (of things like electricity, gas, and oil), overharvesting of animals for food and products including leather goods, cutting down too many trees, and overdevelopment that deprives animals of their natural habitats are all things that are hurting animals and the world around us. Here are some animals that scientists worry may soon go the way of the dinosaurs.

Oceanic whitetip sharks are killed for their huge fins. Their population has declined substantially in the past 50 years.

Hawksbill turtles are threatened because their nesting grounds are destroyed by home construction and their shells are used for jewelry and other items.

African elephants may become extinct if they are not protected; their herds have been reduced by up to 80 percent.

Orangutan habitats are being destroyed to make room for agriculture—such as growing palm trees for oil—and to harvest wood for products.

DINO DETAILS

17 THICK-HEADED LIZARDS MARGINOCEPHALIANS

THICK-HEADED LIZARDS	SIZE	AGE	FOSSILS	LOCATION
Acrotholus (ak-roh-**THOH**-luss)	XS	LC	🦴	NA
Alaskacephale (uh-la-ska-**SEFF**-uh-lee)	S	LC	🦴	NA
Amtocephale (am-toe-**SEFF**-uh-lee)	UN	LC	🦴	AS
Colepiocephale (co-lee-pee-oh-**SEFF**-uh-lee)	XS	LC	🦴	NA
Dracorex (**DRAY**-co-rex)	S	LC	🦴🦴	NA
Goyocephale (go-yoh-**SEFF**-uh-lee)	S	LC	🦴🦴	AS
Gravitholus (**GRA**-vih-thoh-lus)	S	LC	🦴	NA
Hanssuesia (hons-**SUE**-see-a)	S	LC	🦴🦴	NA
Homalocephale (ho-muh-loh-**seff**-uh-lee)	S	LC	🦴	AS

	SIZE	AGE	FOSSILS	LOCATION
Pachycephalosaurus (pak-ih-seff-uh-loh-**SORE**-us)	M	LC	🦴	NA
Prenocephale (pree-no-**SEFF**-uh-lee)	S	LC	🦴🦴	NA/AS
Sphaerotholus (sfee-roh-**THOH**-luss)	S	LC	🦴	NA
Stegoceras (steh-**goss**-er-us)	S	LC	🦴	NA
Stygimoloch (**STIH**-ghee-**MOLL**-uk)	S	LC	🦴	NA
Texacephale (tex-uh-**SEFF**-uh-lee)	S	LC	🦴	NA
Tylocephale (ty-low-**SEFF**-uh-lee)	S	LC	🦴	AS
Wannanosaurus (wah-nah-no-**SORE**-us)	XS	LC	🦴🦴	AS

Homalocephale

Thick-Headed Lizards
Marginocephalians

Dracorex

The skulls of thick-headed dinosaurs such as *Pachycephalosaurus* were covered with tight bony domes. There is little evidence that these domes were used against predators, but the fact that they had them at all indicates that they were useful. Paleontologists think the domes were used to butt one another's flanks when competing for mates.

Dome Heads

Close relatives of dinosaurs with horns and frills, thick-headed dinosaurs had substantial bony domes at the tops of their skulls. They were smaller than their relatives, reaching only 15 feet at their longest. They appeared in the Late Cretaceous period and were mostly found in western North America, as far east as New Mexico, and some have been found in Asia.

PACHYCEPHALOSAURUS

➡ A bipedal herbivore, found in western North America

➡ Name means "thick-headed lizard" in Greek

➡ Was 15 feet long; weighed up to 1,000 pounds

➡ Had a bony skull that was about 10 inches thick

FUN FACT *Pachycephalosaurus* may have used its thick skull to head-butt rivals and predators.

DINO DETECTIVE

RESEARCH

Paleontologists work in labs where experts in different fields can perform tests on bone density and weight and take measurements and pictures, such as X-rays, CT scans, and MRIs. Paleontologists also search through books and computer files that show images of similar bones. People who are not professionals can do research on dinosaurs in other ways—by reading books and news articles, and by visiting museums and dinosaur parks where they can see fossils and skeletons that paleontologists have found.

STEGOCERAS

→ A bipedal herbivore with a 3-inch-thick domed skull

→ Name means "horned roof" in Greek

→ Was 7 feet long; weighed 100–150 pounds

→ Had five clawed fingers on each hand and three clawed toes on each foot

FUN FACT Large, forward-facing eye sockets suggest that *Stegoceras* had binocular vision, to help it focus and see things that were far away.

WHAT'S IN A NAME?

Stego means "roof" or "covering" and *ceras* means "horn" in Greek, so *Stegoceras* means "horned roof"; the top (or roof) of its head was covered in a hornlike material. *Stegosaurus* means "roof lizard"—until a full skeleton was found, experts thought its bony plates were arranged on its back like shingles on a roof. They later learned that the plates stuck out from its back, but by then the name was set.

PRENOCEPHALE

→ A bipedal herbivore with a large skull

→ Name means "sloping head" in Greek

→ Was 7–8 feet long; weighed 200–300 pounds

→ Had a large skull covered with bumps, spikes, and ridges

FUN FACT Only skulls and a few bones have been found, so *Prenocephale* remains a mystery.

Dinosaurs were the dominant creatures during the Jurassic and Cretaceous periods, but they shared Earth with many other animals.

Dinosaurs descended from early reptiles called archosaurs. These reptiles were also the ancestors of crocodiles and birds. During the Age of Dinosaurs, there were huge populations of reptiles, fish, and insects. There were mammals, too, but they were small and barely resembled most of the mammals we know today. Birds evolved from theropod dinosaurs during the Jurassic period.

After dinosaurs became extinct, other life-forms—including bigger mammals—appeared. Some of these later prehistoric creatures were still around when the earliest human forms evolved.

TIMELINE

PALEOZOIC ERA

MESOZOIC ERA

530 TO 400
MILLION YEARS AGO
The earliest jawless fish appeared. Later fish had jaws. Primitive insects appeared.

300
MILLION YEARS AGO
The first reptiles appeared, then grew much bigger. Insects became more advanced.

252
MILLION YEARS AGO
A mass extinction occurred, and 90 percent of ocean creatures and 75 percent of land creatures became extinct.

252 TO 201
MILLION YEARS AGO
TRIASSIC PERIOD:
The first dinosaurs appeared, and marine reptiles thrived.

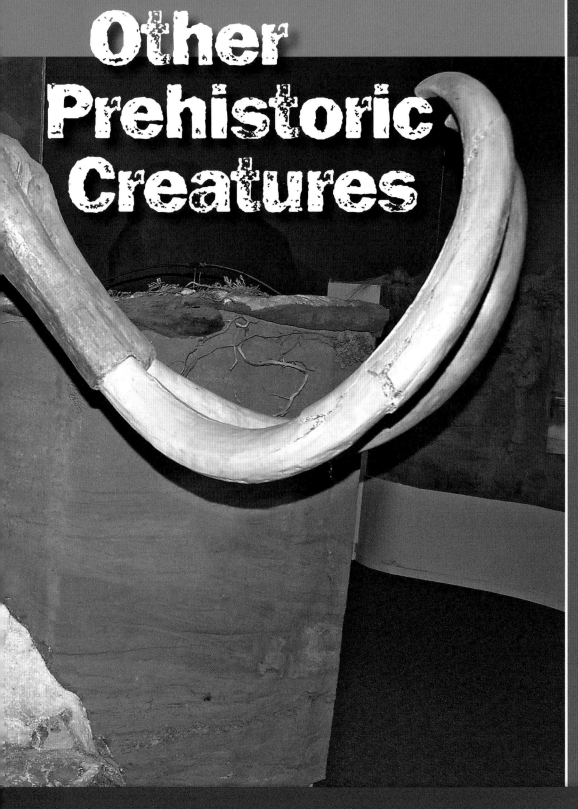

Other Prehistoric Creatures

AT A GLANCE

All forms of animal life existed during the Age of Dinosaurs. Some fish, reptiles, and insects came before dinosaurs and also lived after them. Mammals developed more after the dinosaurs vanished. Birds descended from dinosaurs and still thrive today.

Other prehistoric animals are divided into five sections in this book:

Insects
➤ Included hundreds of species
➤ Of note were cockroaches and butterflies

Fish
➤ Were the first vertebrates
➤ The earliest ones were small and jawless

Reptiles and Amphibians
➤ Lived in the oceans; some evolved to walk on land
➤ Dinosaurs descended from reptiles

Mammals
➤ Were small during the Age of Dinosaurs
➤ Huge versions appeared after dinosaurs became extinct

Birds
➤ Descended from dinosaurs
➤ Included "terror birds" in the Cenozoic era

CENOZOIC ERA

201 TO 144 MILLION YEARS AGO

JURASSIC PERIOD: Huge dinosaurs dominated. Small, furry mammals coexisted with them.

144 TO 66 MILLION YEARS AGO

CRETACEOUS PERIOD: Flowering plants appeared, and birds, mammals, turtles, and crocodiles evolved into more modern forms.

66 MILLION YEARS AGO

Another mass extinction occurred. A large percentage of species—and all dinosaurs—became extinct.

66 MILLION YEARS AGO TO PRESENT

Mammals and birds grew larger. Primitive humans appeared well into this era. The Cenozoic era is still ongoing.

Around 300 million years ago, the amount of oxygen in Earth's atmosphere increased dramatically. Scientists think this was because more plants were growing and giving off oxygen through photosynthesis (the process by which plants create food and oxygen from sunlight and carbon dioxide). The air had 50 percent more oxygen in prehistoric times than it does today.

Insects don't breathe the way we do—they absorb oxygen through their bodies. When there is more oxygen in the atmosphere, they absorb more. So when there was more oxygen in the atmosphere 300 million years ago, insects grew larger and increased in number and variety. Dragonflies, beetles, spiders, butterflies, centipedes, and cockroaches—most of the insects we know today—were around, in some form, during the Age of Dinosaurs. Millions of years later, when oxygen levels dropped, insects could no longer maintain their giant sizes. They evolved into the smaller ones we know today.

TRAPPED IN AMBER

Insects—even giant ones—have very fragile bodies and superthin wings; they can't survive the normal fossilization process. But many insects were preserved in amber, the sap of evergreen trees. When an insect fell into the sticky substance, it got stuck. The sap hardened and turned a deep gold color. Today we can study insects that were preserved this way.

Prehistoric mosquito, preserved in amber

GIANT ANTS Ants date back 50 million years; fossils of 1-inch-long worker ants and 2-inch-long queen ants have been found throughout Europe and North America.

COCKROACHES Fossils of 6-inch-long cockroaches, looking much like the smaller ones we see today, were found in a mine in Ohio. Roaches have been abundant throughout the world for the past 400 million years.

FEATURED CREATURE

GIANT DRAGONFLY

SCIENTIFIC NAME
Meganeura

PRONUNCIATION
*Meg-guh-**NYUR**-uh*

SIZE
2–2.5-foot wingspan

AGE
Early Triassic

LOCATION
Europe

DIET
Other insects

The next time you're buzzed by a helicopter-like dragonfly, imagine how you would feel if it had wings as long as your arm, like the giant dragonfly of prehistoric times did.

PREHISTORIC BUTTERFLIES Butterflies first appeared in the Cretaceous period, around the same time as flowering plants, but the fossils that survived are only fragments. More species appeared about 50 million years ago, and those are very similar to modern butterflies.

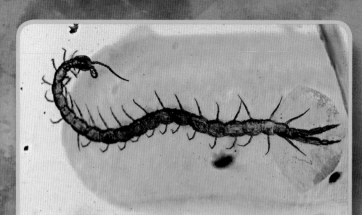

GIANT CENTIPEDES Fossils of bugs similar to modern centipedes have been found in northeastern North America and Scotland. They were 8 feet long and herbivorous.

Life, in its most primitive forms, began in water, so it's not surprising that the first advanced creatures appeared in the oceans. The first fish, which were also the first vertebrates, date back 530 million years. Many fish died at the same time that dinosaurs became extinct. Sharks were particularly affected—thousands of species disappeared. But many kinds of fish, including some sharks, lived on after dinosaurs became extinct. Some are still living today, largely unchanged from their prehistoric forms.

DID YOU KNOW?

During prehistoric times, oceans flowed over regions that are now dry land. That's why fish fossils and teeth are found in landlocked areas.

FEATURED CREATURE

MEGALODON

SCIENTIFIC NAME
Megalodon

PRONUNCIATION
MEG-uh-luh-don

SIZE
50 feet long or more

AGE
Cenozoic, 30–2 million years ago

LOCATION
Worldwide

DIET
Fish, shellfish, whales, and other marine mammals

Megalodon had 7-inch-long teeth and was the ocean's apex predator. It was three times longer than most great whites, and some scientists think that the largest ones may have reached 50 feet or more.

AMMONITES AND OTHER INVERTEBRATES

Fish weren't the only living things in the seas. Invertebrates were plentiful. Ammonites were squid relatives that lived before and during the Age of Dinosaurs and became extinct at the same time. Ammonite shells fossilized easily, and today they give paleontologists a good idea of when certain rocks were formed.

BONES OR NO BONES

Some fish have bones; some have only cartilage (a flexible substance that provides body structure). Fish that have only cartilage—sharks, for example—don't leave skeletons behind, because cartilage dissolves in water over time. But they leave behind teeth and jawbones, which can become fossilized. From these, thousands of species of sharks and other fish have been identified.

Dunkleosteus, a 30-foot-long fish with a primitive but very powerful jaw, lived about 380 million years ago.

FIRST FISH

Early fish were jawless, but had gills that allowed them to breathe underwater. Over the next few hundred million years, fish developed fins, powerful jaws, and hydrodynamic bodies (bodies adapted to moving through water) that helped them survive in the ocean environment.

On Land and in the Sea

Dinosaurs were reptiles, but they weren't the only prehistoric reptiles. Earth teemed with many varieties of prehistoric snakes, crocodiles, lizards, and turtles, as well as many amphibians, including frogs. Many reptiles grew larger than their modern counterparts and developed unusual appendages.

FEATURED CREATURE

DEVIL FROG

SCIENTIFIC NAME
Beelzebufo

PRONUNCIATION
beel-*zeh*-**BOO**-*foh*

SIZE
16 inches long

AGE
Late Cretaceous

LOCATION
Madagascar

DIET
Meat

Dimetrodon, a 10-foot-long reptile, had a big mouth and could swallow other reptiles whole. *Dimetrodon*'s most distinctive feature was a huge sail on its back. Scientists think that mammals descended from *Dimetrodon* and other reptiles like it.

At more than 9 pounds, the devil frog was three times bigger than any modern frog. Its mouth was large enough that it could feed on small dinosaurs.

Archelon, the largest sea turtle ever documented, lived in the Late Cretaceous period.

TURTLES Growing to 12 feet long and weighing up to 2,000 pounds, prehistoric turtles moved quickly and ate by crushing all kinds of food with their hard beaks. Other than their size, turtles that lived during the Triassic period were similar to today's turtles and tortoises.

Protosuchus lived during the Early Jurassic period. Its name means "first crocodile," and it was one of earliest crocodile-like animals.

CROCODILES Crocodiles descended from archosaur ancestors, just like dinosaurs did, but their jaws were longer than dinosaurs' were. In the Jurassic period, they walked on four legs rather than crawled, and many lived on land. Some were small and ate plants; others were carnivores that were able to chew their food like mammals did. The carnivorous crocodiles were among the deadliest predators during the Age of Dinosaurs.

Sanajeh, an 11-foot snake from the Late Cretaceous period, ate eggs and hatchlings of sauropod dinosaurs.

PREHISTORIC SNAKES There is evidence that snakes existed during the Jurassic period, but we know more about the snakes that appeared during the Cretaceous period, when at least four different types lived in the Middle East and South America. They had the same sharp fangs as today's snakes. Later, in the Cenozoic era, huge snakes—up to 35 feet long—slithered through forests and deserts.

Mammals came later than insects, fish, and reptiles. They began to evolve from reptiles by the beginning of the Triassic period; they were small, furry creatures that looked—and scurried about—like mice. Large meat-eating dinosaurs usually ignored them because they weren't meaty enough. These small animals were able to survive because they foraged at night and stayed out of the way of the dinosaurs. For the next hundred million years or so, most mammals stayed small.

SURVIVAL OF THE SMALLEST

When dinosaurs vanished 66 million years ago, many small mammals survived. Scientists believe that because they were so small, they could live on very little food. They could also escape heat by burrowing into the ground. Shown here, *Pseudotribos*, an early mammal from the Middle Jurassic period, was less than 5 inches long.

FEATURED CREATURE

WOOLLY MAMMOTH

SCIENTIFIC NAME

Mammuthus

PRONUNCIATION

MAM-uh-thuss

SIZE

12 feet long

AGE

Cenozoic, 200,000–10,000 years ago

LOCATION

Asia and Alaska

DIET

Grasses and sedges

Relatives of modern elephants, mammoths had curved tusks and grew to immense sizes. They died out around the end of the Ice Age, in part due to the spread of humans across the globe and hunting.

BIGGER AND BIGGER

After the dinosaurs disappeared, mammals grew larger and larger. Giant forms of elephants, tigers, bears, and whales lived between 66 million years ago and 10,000 years ago. Some of these huge mammals died when the Ice Age reduced the amount of food available. Their populations also decreased due to hunting by humans. But in many cases, their descendants lived on in smaller forms.

Glyptodon, the giant armadillo, had bands of bony armor all over its rounded shell. It lived 2 million years ago to 10,000 years ago.

Smilodon, the saber-toothed tiger, lived 2.5 million years ago to 10,000 years ago. It hunted large herbivores and is known for its curved front teeth.

Diprotodon, the giant wombat, was the largest marsupial ever. An herbivore, it lived 1.6 million years ago to 46,000 years ago.

Indricotherium, a rhinoceros-like mammal, was 18 feet tall and weighed 34,000 pounds. It lived 32 million years ago to 23 million years ago.

THE FIRST HUMANS

As mammals grew bigger, a new type of animal closely related to apes evolved around 200,000 years ago. This new mammal had a large, well-developed brain that made it able to create and use tools and to communicate with other members of its species. For the next couple hundred thousand years, it evolved further to become more sophisticated. 40,000 years ago, primitive humans began to record history, and modern human beings appeared about 10,000 years ago.

Birds and dinosaurs are closely related. Scientists have debated for many years exactly what this connection is; they now agree that birds descended from theropod dinosaurs. One of the earliest flying creatures was *Archaeopteryx*, the first bird, but no one is sure whether *Archaeopteryx* was the ancestor of modern birds. Paleontologists are still searching for early birds and more clues about their evolution from theropod dinosaurs.

PTEROSAURS (*TERR-uh*-sores) lived from the Late Triassic period to the Late Cretaceous period and are considered to be the first vertebrates capable of powered flight. They weren't birds—they were flying reptiles. They moved through the air by extending superlong fingers that formed membranous wings.

FEATURED CREATURE

QUETZALCOATLUS

SCIENTIFIC NAME
Quetzalcoatlus

PRONUNCIATION
kwet-*sal*-**KOH**-at-*lus*

SIZE
35-foot wingspan

AGE
Late Cretaceous

LOCATION
Southwestern United States and Mexico

DIET
Fish, possibly meat

This huge pterosaur had the longest wingspan of any flying creature and was named after the Aztec feathered snake god.

TERROR BIRDS

A few million years after dinosaurs became extinct—about 62 million years ago—flightless birds called phorusrhacids (*FOR-us-rass-kids*) were apex predators in the region that now encompasses South America, Central America, Mexico, and the southwestern United States. They had no teeth, but their beaks were hard and their necks were strong, so they held their prey down with sharp talons and pecked them to death. They lived from 60 million years ago until 2.5 million years ago and are known in folklore as "terror birds."

DR. JOE SAYS

For centuries, the origins of birds were a mystery to scientists. Several scientists, including Charles Darwin, theorized that birds were a type of reptile and that they once had sharp teeth and long, bony tails. The discovery of the early bird *Archaeopteryx* confirmed their theories, but the exact origins were still a mystery. With the recent discoveries of feathers, nesting behavior, and similar bone structures in the meat-eating theropod dinosaurs, scientists now agree that birds are a specialized type of dinosaur that survived the extinction 66 million years ago. The next time you sit down to eat a turkey sandwich, you will actually be eating a dinosaur sandwich!

— *Dr. Joseph Sertich,*
Paleontologist

The Survivors

Several large extinctions have occurred over the 4.6 billion years of Earth's existence, and each killed off most, but not all, creatures alive at the time. Why did some animal species survive when so many others died off? The survivors were probably well adapted to their environment, and their environment offered protection from catastrophes that killed off other species. Most of these survivors lived in water and were generalists, meaning they could survive on a variety of foods or in a variety of conditions.

Horseshoe crabs have lived near coastlines all around the world for about 445 million years. What makes them such good survivors? They have blood that fights bacteria; the medical industry is studying it to see if it can be beneficial to humans.

Animals like the nautilus have been around for more than 500 million years. These mollusks, related to the squid and octopus, are efficient at finding food. They are facing a challenge to survival: People collect them for their pretty shells, which is causing their population to dwindle.

Great white sharks have amazingly efficient bodies and high intelligence—some of the traits that make them apex predators in their ocean environment. Their ancestors swam the oceans long before the Age of Dinosaurs.

Lamprey eels have small mouths filled with sharp teeth, but they lack jaws. They can attach their mouths to other fish and suck their blood. It's a system which to that has worked for them for more than 300 million years.

There are animals on Earth today that have changed very little over hundreds of millions of years. The ancestors of these animal species lived during the Age of Dinosaurs.

The tuatara, which lives only in New Zealand, is a small reptile that has had the same body structure for the past 220 million years. It survived when the rest of its order became extinct. Many of its relatives lived with the dinosaurs during the Jurassic period.

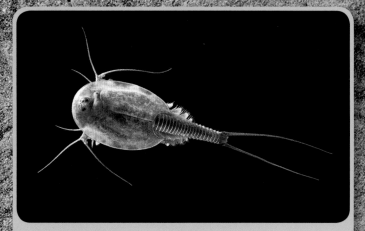

Tadpole shrimp, also called *Triops*, have stayed the same since the Triassic period. At that time, they developed the ability to actively search for food on the ocean floor instead of eating only what floated into their mouths.

Coelacanths, thought to have become extinct at the end of the Age of Dinosaurs, were discovered off South Africa in 1938. They have a unique anatomical feature—they can lift the top part of their head to open wide for feeding.

Alligator gars are 10-foot-long fish that have been in existence for more than 150 million years. They have long, crocodile-shaped jaws. They hunt by staying still and ambushing their prey.

There are more than 750 "named," or officially recognized, dinosaur species, and that number is constantly changing. New discoveries are made every year, and, as experts learn more about them, some dinosaurs that have been named are found to be variations of already known dinosaurs. Others are brand-new additions to the list. Scientists estimate—based on frequency of finds—that only a tiny percentage of the dinosaurs that lived have been found so far.

HOW DOES A NEW DINOSAUR BECOME "NAMED"?

When the bones of a dinosaur are discovered—whether by professional paleontologists on a dig or by amateurs—scientists analyze them carefully and describe them in great detail. They compare them to the bones of dinosaurs that are already known to see if they are different enough to be considered a new genus. If the differences are significant—even if they are small differences—the scientists give them new names, write articles about the discovery, and publish them in scientific journals. It can sometimes take years of study before a new discovery is confirmed and named, and there is sometimes a lot of debate about whether a discovery is truly a new dinosaur.

PINOCCHIO REX

In the spring of 2014, paleontologists in China unearthed a smaller cousin of *T. rex* that had a long snout; they officially named it *Qianzhousaurus*, but commonly call it "Pinocchio rex" after its long nose. A theropod tyrannosaur like *T. rex*, it was about 29 feet long—*T. rex* was more than 40 feet long.

Every year, new dinosaurs are discovered. The number of known dinosaurs has more than doubled in the past 25 years, and the total keeps growing.

THE BIGGEST DINOSAUR

In May 2014, paleontologists working in the Patagonia region of Argentina announced that they had found fossils of the biggest dinosaur that ever lived. Its size was estimated at 130 feet long, and weight at 156,000 pounds. If confirmed, this titanosaur, a type of sauropod, will take the top spot away from *Argentinosaurus*, also found in South America.

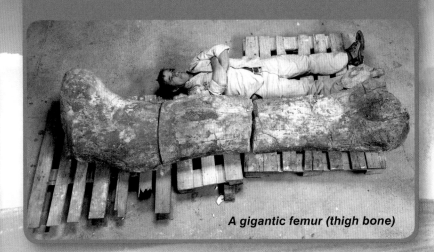

A gigantic femur (thigh bone)

DR. JOE SAYS

In 2007, Andy Farke and I headed to Madagascar to look for new dinosaurs. We got lucky and noticed a couple of bones peeking out of a sandy cliff. The bones turned out to be seven vertebrae and a couple of ribs from a small theropod dinosaur. We suspected it was a new species because no dinosaurs from its time period had ever been discovered in this area. It took four more years of work comparing the vertebrae to other closely related species for us to be sure. In the end, we named it, a new species of abelisaur theropod dinosaur, *Dahalokely tokana*. The name means "lonely little bandit," and refers to the fact that Madagascar was a separate island by the time *Dahalokely* arrived on the scene.

— *Dr. Joseph Sertich, Paleontologist*

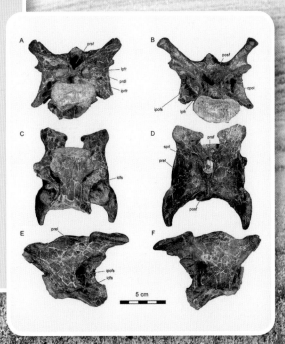

The U.S. National Parks Service celebrates National Fossil Day each year in October. Talk to your teacher about creating a fossil day in your classroom. You could do these activities at home, too.

TALK TO AN EXPERT

Ask a trusted adult to help you find someone in your area who knows a lot about fossils. It might be someone who works at a local museum, a person at an agricultural extension office who works with soil and rocks, or an instructor who teaches at a nearby university. Ask the expert to talk to your class, scout troop, or group of dino-loving friends. The expert might even be able to bring some fossils you can touch and talk about. Be sure to think of good questions to ask before you meet the expert and write them down. Experts love to show their knowledge by answering thoughtful questions.

YOUNG PALEONTOLOGISTS APPLY WITHIN

Many natural history museums have special programs for young people. Check the websites of museums and nature parks you visit (you'll find some great ones in the resources section of this book). For instance, Dr. Joe's Denver Museum of Nature & Science has a junior paleontologist program for students to learn hands-on in the museum and then take materials back to the classroom or home for further study.

PLAN A PALEO PARTY

➡ Invite friends and family to a party with a special dino invitation. Copy one of the dinosaurs at left or draw your own. Add information about where and when your party will take place. Don't forget to include a specific location with a date and time.

➡ Make up dinosaur name tags for all of your guests with a different species on each one. Have your book ready so everyone can look up their dinosaur and find out all about its behavior.

➡ Serve a buffet fit for huge reptiles! Arrange your party food into categories for herbivores, carnivores, and omnivores. (You can skip the insectivore platter.)

➡ A fun way to decorate your buffet table is to make your own fossil. Roll out art clay and use a toy dinosaur to make footprint fossils. Find some small leaves and press them firmly into clay to make leaf fossils.

MATERIALS NEEDED:

• Construction paper or card stock, markers, and scissors for invitations

• Paper, scissors, crayons, tape for name tags

• Delicious treats such as a fruit and veggie platter, fish sticks and chicken fingers, pizza with both vegetables and pepperoni

• Modeling clay to making fossils

DESIGN A DINO

Imagine you are on a dig and discover a totally new dinosaur.

After answering the following questions, choose a name for your dinosaur, and draw its picture. If you're doing this activity with a friend or brother or sister, ask them to describe their dinosaurs, too. Make a game of it!

➡ What kind of fossils did you find?

➡ How big are the fossils? What size is the dinosaur they belonged to? How tall? How heavy?

➡ Did you find a skull? Do the eyes face forward or are they on the side of the head?

➡ How about the teeth? Are they sharp or dull? Can the teeth tell you if the dinosaur is a carnivore or an herbivore?

➡ How big are the legs? Did it walk on two feet or four feet?

➡ How long are its neck and tail?

➡ Did you find fossilized skin or skin impressions that give a clue as to the color of the skin? Was the skin bumpy or smooth?

➡ Did your dinosaur have special features such as a crest or a club on its tail?

➡ What about feathers or body armor?

➡ What is your dinosaur's name?

MATERIALS NEEDED:
Paper, pencils, markers, and crayons for drawing or paints for painting

PUPPET SHOW!

Take your drawing one step further—and more fun. Cut out your dinosaur picture and tape it to a Popsicle stick or unsharpened pencil to make a puppet. Have a friend do the same. Now you can stage a show. It's easy to make a puppet theater by draping a blanket over a table. Duck behind the table and have your puppets "walk" on the back edge. You might even try writing some dialogue for your big performance.

ON THE SCENE

Now that you have created your own dinosaur, you can put it into action.

Imagine your dinosaur in its habitat. Think about how it moves and looks for food.

Decide where your dinosaur lives. Does it live in a desert, a swamp, or a forest?

Now imagine that another dinosaur comes into the scene. Is your dinosaur a carnivore that will attack? Or is your dinosaur an herbivore that must defend itself?

Write the story you have imagined, describing both dinosaurs and the habitat in which they meet. If there is a battle, who wins?

MATERIALS NEEDED:
Paper and pencil, or computer or tablet

MUSEUMS AND EXHIBITS

CALIFORNIA

Natural History Museum of Los Angeles County
900 Exposition Blvd.
Los Angeles, CA 90007
nhm.org

The museum's Dinosaur Institute houses thousands of fossils, including three T. rex skeletons, a Triceratops, and a Mamenchisaurus.

University of California Museum of Paleontology
1101 Valley Life Sciences Bldg.
Berkeley, CA 94720
ucmp.berkeley.edu

This is the largest collection of fossils at any university museum in the world. It houses some exhibits open to the public, including complete skeletons of a T. rex and a Pteranodon.

San Diego Natural History Museum
1788 El Prado, Balboa Park
San Diego, CA 92101
sdnhm.org

Tour 75 million years of the fossil history of Southern California at "theNAT" and see a Nodosaurus and a full Allosaurus reconstruction, as well as Fossil Mysteries.

COLORADO

Dinosaur Journey Museum Museum of Western Colorado
550 Jurassic Ct.
Fruita, CO 81521
museumofwesternco.com/visit/dinosaur-journey/

This building houses a Velociraptor and a Stegosaurus, as well as many other skeletons.

Denver Museum of Nature & Science
2001 Colorado Blvd.
Denver, CO 80205
dmns.org

Dr. Joseph Sertich—our Dr. Joe—is Curator of Vertebrate Paleontology at this major research and educational institution. Visitors can watch a Stegosaurus battle an Allosaurus as a Diplodocus towers overhead, examine fossils from Touch Carts, feel how Earth warmed and cooled in prehistoric times, and see the largest volunteer-led dinosaur lab in the world.

CONNECTICUT

Yale Peabody Museum of Natural History
170 Whitney Ave.
New Haven, CT 06511
peabody.yale.edu

This museum was founded by the uncle of the famous paleontologist O. C. Marsh, and many of his discoveries, including a Triceratops, a Stegosaurus, and a Brontosaurus (now Apatosaurus) are displayed in the museum.

GEORGIA

Fernbank Museum of Natural History
767 Clifton Rd. NE
Atlanta, GA 30307
fernbankmuseum.org

The Giants of the Mesozoic exhibit features a Giganotosaurus, a large carnivore; an Argentinosaurus, the longest herbivore; and 20 pterosaurs flying overhead.

ILLINOIS

The Field Museum
1400 S. Lake Shore Dr.
Chicago, IL 60605
fieldmuseum.org

In addition to the T. rex Sue, the Field Museum houses the Genius Hall of Dinosaurs, where specimens from every dinosaur group are displayed. The Evolving Planet exhibit features dinosaurs from different periods and from locations around the globe.

KANSAS

Museum of World Treasures
835 E. 1st St.
Wichita, KS 67202
worldtreasures.org

Skeletons of a T. rex, an Edmontosaurus, and other dinosaurs are displayed in a battle scene at this Midwest museum.

MINNESOTA

Science Museum of Minnesota
120 W. Kellogg Blvd.
St. Paul, MN 55102
smm.org

A Triceratops, a Diplodocus, an Allosaurus, a Stegosaurus, and a Camptosaurus are among the real and replicated skeletons featured in the Dinosaurs and Fossils Gallery.

MONTANA

Museum of the Rockies
600 W. Kagy Blvd.
Bozeman, MT 59717
museumoftherockies.org

This museum is the scientific home of Dr. John R. "Jack" Horner, who discovered the Maiasaura nests; his finds are housed there, amid displays and re-creations that showcase dinosaur behavior.

NEW YORK

American Museum of Natural History
Central Park W. & 79th St.
New York, NY 10024
amnh.org

In four grand halls and vast storage areas, the world's largest collection of vertebrate fossils—nearly 1 million items—is catalogued and displayed for both professionals and the public. A five-story-tall Barosaurus, an Apatosaurus, the first Velociraptor skull ever found, and a mummified hadrosaur are just a few of the attractions to be seen.

PENNSYLVANIA

The Academy of Natural Sciences of Drexel University
1900 Benjamin Franklin Pkwy.
Philadelphia, PA 19103
ansp.org

A dig pit and animated environments are new features in the oldest science museum in the United States. A Hadrosaurus (the first nearly complete dinosaur skeleton ever found) and a Gigantoraptor (the largest carnivore ever found) are displayed in the museum's dinosaur hall.

Carnegie Museum of Natural History
4400 Forbes Ave.
Pittsburgh, PA 15213
carnegiemnh.org

Nineteen dinosaurs are exhibited in re-created environments that show the differences between the Triassic, Jurassic, and Cretaceous periods. At the Bonehunters Quarry, an interactive fossil dig re-creation, kids can use chisels and brushes to uncover realistic fossil casts.

TEXAS

Houston Museum of Natural Science
5555 Hermann Park Dr.
Houston, TX 77030
hmns.org

Dinosaurs are arranged in scenes that show how they lived—eating, fighting, escaping predators. A prehistoric safari reveals the evolution of dinosaurs. "Al," a juvenile Allosaurus, *is one of this museum's highlights.*

Perot Museum of Nature and Science
2201 N. Field St.
Dallas, TX 75201
perotmuseum.org

Huge dinosaur skeletons, including a Mamenchisaurus, *are on display, along with interactive exhibits on topics such as eggs, evolution, and dinosaur eating habits.*

UTAH

Natural History Museum of Utah
301 Wakara Way
Salt Lake City, UT 84108
nhmu.utah.edu

More than 30 skeletons are displayed, including a Gryposaurus *(a duck-billed dinosaur) and 14 ceratopsians. Visitors can be paleontologists for a day in a dinosaur dig.*

WASHINGTON, D.C.

Smithsonian National Museum of Natural History
10th St. & Constitution Ave. NW
Washington, DC 20560
naturalhistory.si.edu

The National Fossil Hall, which housed the dinosaur exhibit at this free museum, closed for renovations in 2014. However, dinosaur exhibits can be found elsewhere in the museum, including in the Rex Room (where visitors can observe scientists working on T. rex *bones).*

WISCONSIN

Dinosaur Discovery Museum
5608 10th Ave.
Kenosha, WI 53140
kenosha.org/wp-dinosaur

The only museum to focus on the link between theropod dinosaurs and birds, this museum presents current research that shows the evolutionary transitions.

WYOMING

The Wyoming Dinosaur Center
110 Carter Ranch Rd.
Thermopolis, WY 82443
wyodino.org

In 12,000 square feet of exhibit space, this museum displays 20 full-size dinosaur skeletons, including a 106-foot Supersaurus. *Outside the museum, visitors can tour Warm Springs Ranch, home to over 60 dig sites.*

CANADA

Royal Tyrrell Museum
Hwy. 838
Drumheller, AB T0J 0Y0
tyrrellmuseum.com

In addition to more than 130,000 fossils, and nine galleries full of dinosaur skeletons (including "Black Beauty," a T. rex *with dark bones, and a pack of* Albertosauruses), *this important museum presents interactive displays and a preparation lab where visitors can watch paleontologists work on fossilized bones.*

NATIONAL, STATE, AND PROVINCIAL PARKS

COLORADO/UTAH

Dinosaur National Monument
4545 U.S. 40
Dinosaur, CO 81610
nps.gov/dino

Dinosaurs once roamed freely in this area, and the deserts, mountains, and canyons of this park are rich with fossils. Visitors can view about 1,500 dinosaur bones and the remains of an Allosaurus, *an* Apatosaurus, *a* Camarasaurus, *a* Diplodocus, *and a* Stegosaurus. *You can even touch 149-million-year-old dinosaur bones!*

CONNECTICUT

Dinosaur State Park
400 West St.
Rocky Hill, CT 06067
dinosaurstatepark.org

A dome covers one the largest and best-preserved dinosaur trackways in the country. The park is full of nature trails and information markers that allow visitors to understand what this landscape looked like in prehistoric times.

CANADA

Dinosaur Provincial Park
Brooks, AB T0J 2K0
albertaparks.ca/dinosaur.aspx

More than 40 dinosaurs were discovered in this park, located in Canada's badlands. The park displays fossils of more than 500 forms of life, from tiny plants to huge dinosaurs.

BOOKS TO READ

Boy, Were We Wrong About Dinosaurs!
Kathleen V. Kudlinski

Explore all the mistakes that scientists made about dinosaurs—that they were dragons, or that they could float—and the notions we believe today that may one day be proven false.

Digging Dinosaurs: The Search That Unraveled the Mystery of Baby Dinosaurs
John R. Horner and James Gorman

Follow a famous paleontologist as he makes a remarkable discovery that advances our knowledge of how dinosaurs are born.

WEBSITES TO CHECK OUT

ucmp.berkeley.edu/ diapsids/dinobuzz.html

DinoBuzz, from the University of California Museum of Paleontology, covers scientific topics such as warm-bloodedness and extinction in an interesting and fun way.

kidsdigdinos.com

Kids Dig Dinos gathers information about dinosaurs for kids who want to learn more about them. The site is run by kids, who have a good idea of what other kids want to know!

enchantedlearning.com/ subjects/dinosaurs/

Zoom Dinosaurs has information about dinosaur anatomy, behavior, habitats, and fossils. The site includes 93 information pages about individual dinosaurs.

digonsite.com/guide/

Dig magazine's state-by-state guide provides information about digs for kids, families, and schools.

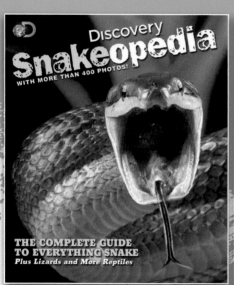
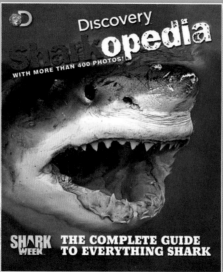